How to Make an Android eBook App

Dr. Mohammed Isam
2016

How to make an Android eBook App.
First Edition, 2016.

ISBN-13: 978-1535242820
ISBN-10: 1535242825

Printed by: CreateSpace, an Amazon.com company.

Available from Amazon.com, CreateSpace.com, and other retail outlets.

Dr. Mohammed Isam Mohammed Abdel-Magid
Phone: +97470445235
E-mail: mohammed_isam1984@yahoo.com
Website: http://sites.google.com/site/mohammedisam2000

Table of Contents

Chapter 1: Introduction

1.1 Why Do I Need This?

Information is everywhere around us. It used to be stored in books, but this is ancient history. Knowledge is nowadays at your fingertips. You can read a book on your tablet, browse an online encyclopedia through your phone's browser, watch a video tutorial on YouTube, and so forth.

This has made the job of delivering information to users a demanding task. You are not obliged to, but your readers would very much appreciate if you could provide the information they need in an easy-to-get format. This is why most publishers now are making effort to provide their published material in different formats, to appeal to the taste of their diverse range of readers.

One of the most popular electronic media for information delivery is through smart phones and tablets. Most readers will settle for reading books and other material using one or more of these devices.

And in the world of smart phones, Android is a big player. It quickly acquired a large sum of the market share. Android is an open source operating system, developed by Google, and is found in virtually every device you can find around you: smart phones, tablets, smart TVs, smart watches, to mention some.

If you are a publisher or an author and you didn't think before of publishing your material for Android users, you have to reconsider it. Think of reaching out to millions of worldwide users who will be very happy to access your material on their hand-held devices. Those users are loyal, and they will most probably continue to update the software they downloaded from your company once they are convinced it is stable, useful and user-friendly. They will even look for other software developed by your company in most cases.

So, if you are a publishing house, a self-publishing author, a maintainer of a public domain book, or even a curious developer, and you want to know how to deploy your book(s) on the Android platform, this book is just for you.

1.2 Is Programming Knowledge Needed?

As I know most readers of this text would not be programmers, or would have a minimal knowledge in programming, I have written this book in a clear and simple instructive way. This is not to give you the idea that this book is an introductory course to programming: *it is not*.

Developing Android programs is exactly that: *developing* programs. That means some amount of programming is due, but don't despair. I wrote this book in a way that will not make you feel the need to go and learn a new programming language. The code snippets are written on a "to-go" basis, i.e. you can copy and paste the code fragments into the editor (with minor modifications that I will show you along the code) and guarantee that they will do the required job, provided of course you follow closely the instructions in this book to get the job done.

The development of our sample book will require the following tasks, which I will detail throughout the text:

1. Downloading and installing the software required for operation.
2. Setting up an SQLite database for the eBook.
3. Writing the code backbone that will drive the application to work.
4. Formatting your manuscript to be ready for incorporation into the database, and thence the App.
5. Minor designing (mainly of the App icons) and your book figures and images.
6. Testing the App on an Android Virtual Device (AVD) and on a real physical device.
7. Registering with Google Play Store as a developer, and publishing the App.
8. Advertising, promoting and recruiting users to use the App.

The last point is the one I will not discuss in this book. This is a job for professionals, and if you are not one of them, you are better off searching for professional help. I will though give you some tips and guidance about where to search for such help.

To reiterate: this book *is not* an introduction to Java programming, nor is it an introduction to Android development. If you want in-depth and more structured information in either of these topics, you must look for another book that gives that information.

This book is a hands-on tutorial on creating an eBook, in the form of an Android App. This is the main focus of the book. Everything else (Java code, XML code, graphics design, Android system internals) are supplementary material to get the job done. I will touch on all those subjects in a superficial way, just like a "refresher" for your brain. If you find a topic that you didn't understand, don't hesitate to search the net or look into another book to get it clear before carrying on.

1.3 Why Not Publish my Book as a Regular eBook?

There are many eBook formats out there. One of the most popular and widely used format is Adobe's PDF (Portable Document Format). PDF is found everywhere. There is very little chance that you might have not encountered PDF somehow during your life and work. PDF was introduced by Adobe in 1993.

PDF is good. It provides a static document view. That means whatever device or software you use to view the document, it should essentially look the same as the original. The problem is that it is *static*, i.e. it doesn't give you much liberty about how to view the document.

Think about this book at your hand. It is composed of pages that contain text and images. If you view this book in a PDF viewer, it will display it almost exactly as I wrote it in the first place. This is satisfactory if you are using a wide screen medium, like a computer or a laptop's screen.

But what if you wanted to view the book on your notebook? Your tablet? Or even the tiny screen of your mobile phone? Wouldn't it be tiresome and boring to keep scrolling to the right to see the rest of the line, then back to the left and down to see the rest of the page?.

This is why other eBook formats were invented, like ePub, Mobi and Google Books. In this case, the book text is saved as regular text, with some meta-data that give information to the viewer application including the author, publisher, fonts used, and other things. The viewer application is then free to format the book into pages that fit the screen resolution and size of the target device. This results in enhanced user experience as the user will no longer have to go back and forth to view a complete page.

There are many companies and websites that can help an author/publisher create eBooks. Those are only examples and the list is by no means inclusive:

1. Amazon Kindle Direct Publishing (https://kdp.amazon.com/).
2. Lulu Press Inc. (http://www.lulu.com/create/ebooks).
3. Nook Press (https://www.nookpress.com/ebooks).
4. Other sites could be searched for by searching for "publishing ebooks" on your search engine.

Most of those sites will give you two options: a free publishing option, where you have to do most of the work yourself, including formatting your manuscript, designing your graphics to make them print- and display-suitable, cover design (Amazon provides an online cover design helper), and so on. The other option is paid publishing, where a team of professionals will help your with the said tasks for a given price.

This is all good, but it still is limited. Amazon Kindle Publishing will publish your books for Amazon Kindle devices. That means your book will not be available for users without those devices (not entirely true, though, as there are Kindle emulators). Other book formats will need an eBook reader in order to view the book on the target device. Many eBook readers are available as both free and paid software.

So, either you limit your reader base to a set of defined users, or bind the user to install an eBook reader, which is a trivial task on most occasions. But there is more.

Books published as eBooks are easy to read. I am not talking about reading the text itself, but reading the formatted eBook file. As most eBook formats are well known (some are even public domain), anyone with enough knowledge could crack the book file wide open and get every bit of data out of it. Why would you want to hide your data? For several reasons actually.

If you are a publisher, you want credit for your business. We all know that book piracy is ever-growing. People are always trying to get paid things for free. In this case, you lose money if your material is leaked without your permission. You might want to restrict users from copying text directly from your book, something that those eBook readers will not provide efficiently for you.

You might want to publish an eMagazine that will be updated regularly to provide the reader with the last articles and news. Publishing an eBook the traditional way will not help you much. You need a way to make your eMagazine query your server on regular intervals to look for new material, download it and show it to the readers.

You might be a self publisher who wants to publish your many books to your readers, but you want them to be grouped in a nice virtual library, where the user can select the book he wants, read it (but not giving it away for his family, friends, and third-grade cousin Jimmy who is vising from out of town), and save the collection in a handy and easy-to-find way.

You might be an author/publisher whose material is written in a right-to-left language like Arabic or Hebrew. The publishing sites I listed above (and those are the big boys) don't give you an option to electronically publish such material. They all work on Latin-based, left-to-right languages. You need to invent your own way of publishing your eBooks.

Those might be some of the reasons why you want to publish your book as a software app. Maybe you have other agenda, like being a programming enthusiast who likes to bend his back for hours in front of a monitor, writing lines and lines of code. Maybe you don't trust third party programmers who will happily format your book, but will steal your credit card information and social security number and ambush you for evil reasons. You might be one of those insane users who hate Apps that pop Ads every 3 seconds on their faces (how insane!). Either way, the experience of developing your book into an application is a fun, rewarding and a worthwhile experience that you will appreciate it if you tried it.

So, to sum up, the pros of taking this journey to build up your own eBook are:

1. Having full control over your App, its contents and what it does, with no third party interference.
2. Building a stand-alone eBook software that is independent of other third party eBook viewers.
3. You books, your material, your eBooks, meaning more business for you and your company.

4. You are free to update, enhance and improve your App with no need to pay a third party development service.
5. You can create the eBooks that online publishers refused to publish, like Arabic and Hebrew material (and text in other, less-supported languages also).
6. It is not that hard to develop an Android App.
7. It is actually fun to develop and Android App.

While the cons include:
1. You will spend some time to understand what's really going on under the hood. You are no longer a regular Android user, you are a developer.
2. It will take time, dedication and effort to produce a secure, stable and a good App. It takes also effort to keep things updated and release follow versions and patches.
3. While you can use this book to build a whole eBook App without knowing a thing about programming and the Android platform, I actually advise you to read some books to gain a better perspective about what's really going on.
4. If you produce a bad App, one that crashes all the time, or one with a pale, ugly user interface, you are going to get bad reviews. Bad reviews means bad reputation, and bad business.

1.4 Order of Business

First things first, we need to set up the development environment for our upcoming venture. The Android toolkit we will use is available under different operating systems (OSes), including MS-Windows, GNU/Linux, and Mac OS X. I am using Fedora Linux 24 Workstation, a popular and widely used distribution (distro) of GNU/Linux for desktop computers. You are not bound to using this particular OS or this specific distro of GNU/Linux. I am mentioning this just to let you know that most of the screenshots you will see through the text are taken on my Fedora Linux box, so it might look a little different on your system. Otherwise, the software should work on any of the above mentioned systems, given they are set up properly.

We will need the following software:

1. Java JDK (Java Development Kit) as Java is the programming language we will use.
2. Android SDK (Software Development Kit) that contains the libraries we will need for developing our app. This is part of the Android Studio Integrated Development Environment (IDE).

1.4.1 Installing JDK

Follow the following steps to get JDK installed and running on your system:

1. Navigate to the Java SE Downloads Page: http://www.oracle.com/technetwork/java/javase/downloads/index.html in your web browser (see Figure 1.1). My snapshot is taken on Firefox, but the page will look the same regardless of your browser.
2. Click on the big icon that says **Java** (with "Java Platform (JDK)" below it).
3. The Java SE Development Kit 8 – Downloads page opens (Figure 1.2). Scroll down to the list of downloads. You will need to select the **Accept License Agreement** radio button in order to enable the download. Select the download that is appropriate according to your OS and your platform. Notice that you need to install the 32-bit (x86) version for developing Android applications. If you are using a 64-bit (x64) machine, you can install both versions.
4. If you are using an RPM-based GNU/Linux (like Fedora, CentOS, OpenSUSE or Redhat Enterprise Linux - RHEL), download the RPM installer (which is easier to install, and will nicely put everything in place). Otherwise you can download the zipped archive (.tar.gz), unpack it somewhere in your directory tree (e.g. under /home/yourname), and follow the instructions in the Installation Guide on http://docs.oracle.com/javase/8/docs/technotes/guides/install/index.html.
5. If you are using GNU/Linux, there is a good chance that JDK is already installed on your system. You can check this by opening a Terminal and typing:

```
java -version
```

Which would return the JDK version if Java is installed.

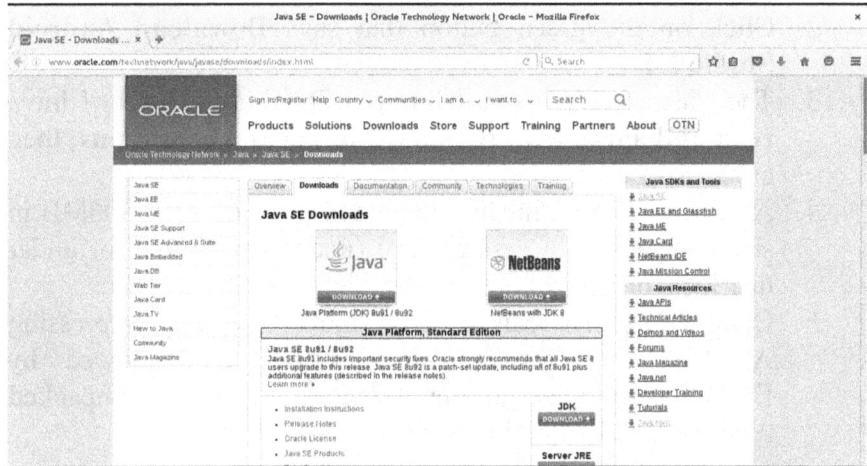

Figure 1.1: Java SE Downloads Page.

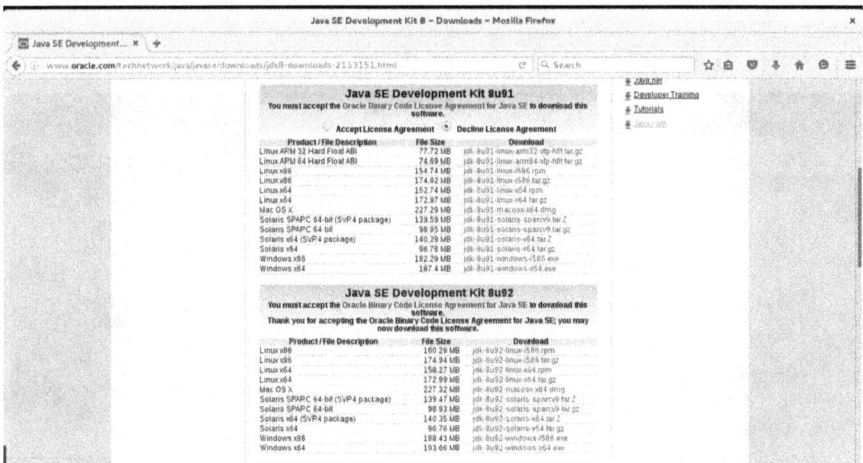

Figure 1.2: Java SE Development Kit 8 – Downloads Page.

1.4.2 Installing Android Studio

The Android SDK contains the essential tools for developing Android apps. It includes a debugger, Android libraries, documentation, sample code, among other tools. This is all packaged

13

in an Integrated Development Environment (IDE) called Android Studio.

To install the Android Studio on your system, follow these steps:

1. Navigate to https://developer.android.com/studio/index.html (Figure 1.3).
2. Click on the green button that says **Download Android Studio 2.1.**
3. The License Agreement tab opens. Read it and select **I have read and agree with the above terms and conditions**, then click Download.
4. After the ZIP file finishes download (it is just over 300MB in size), unpack it in a safe place (under your home, or under /usr/local or /opt).
5. Open a terminal (can be done under GNOME by pressing ALT+F2, then writing `gnome-terminal`, followed by ENTER). Navigate to the directory where you unpacked Android Studio, and invoke:

```
bin/studio.sh
```

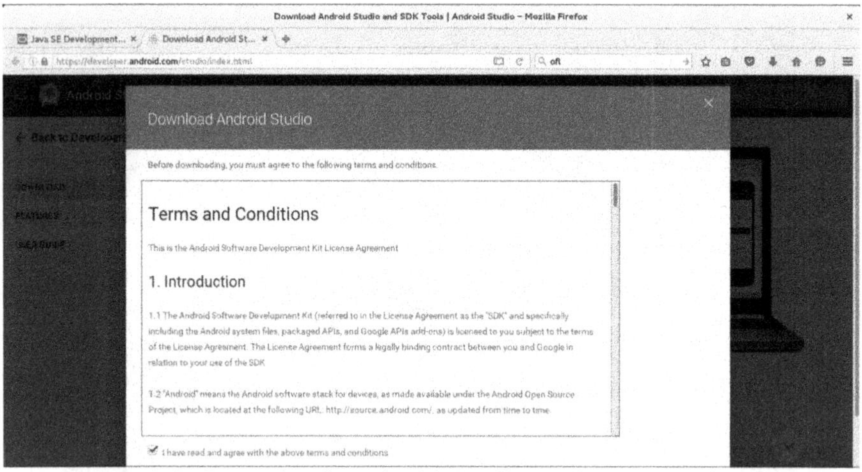

Figure 1.3: Download Android Studio and SDK Tools Page.

6. It will ask you if you had a previous version of Android Studio and whether you want to import settings. You can skip this step and click OK.
7. If you are using Windows, the executable is about 1.2GB in

14

size. After downloading the file, double click it to start the installer. After the installer finishes, open the Android Studio executable.

8. The Android Studio Setup Wizard will give you a welcome screen. Press the **Next** button.
9. Select the Type of Setup. The **Standard** option is enough, so leave it there and click **Next**.
10. In the **SDK Components Setup** screen, the basic items are selected. We will need an **Android Virtual Device** for testing our application later, so tick this item in the left hand-list. In the **Android SDK Location** field at the bottom of the screen, click the button with the three dots, select the folder where you installed the Android SDK in the previous steps, and then click **Next**.
11. Review the settings you have chosen and click **Finish.**
12. Sit back and wait while the Studio downloads and installs the missing components.
13. Meanwhile, you can read the useful instructions provided in the https://developer.android.com/studio/install.html document.

You will want to add the Android tools to your system path, so as to be able to run the Studio from any where. On GNU/Linux, you can simply open a terminal and type:

```
export
$PATH=$PATH:/usr/local/Android/Sdk/tools:/usr/local/A
ndroid/Sdk/platform-tools
```

Of course, you will replace the path **/usr/local/Android/Sdk** with the path where you installed the Android SDK in the steps above.
This effect will not sustain a reboot. In order to make the changes to the PATH variable permanent, you will need to add some lines to the **.bashrc** file (you can use the **.profile** file also) under your home directory. Open a terminal and write:

```
vi ~/.bashrc
```

This will open the Vi text editor. Press **G** (capital letter G) to go to the end of the file. Press **O** (letter O) to open a new line under the current line. Add those two lines:

```
export ANDROID=$HOME/Android/Sdk
export    PATH=$PATH:$ANDROID/tools:$ANDROID/platform-
tools
```

Press ESC to exit the **insert mode** and return to the **command mode**. Press ! (exclamation mark, called a *bang*), then *w* and *q* and press ENTER. This will save the file (w for Write changes) and close the editor (q for Quit). Now when you log in the next time, your path will include the path to the Android SDK tools. You can check this the next time you log in by opening a terminal and typing:

```
echo $PATH
```

You should see the above path at the end of the environment PATH variable.

If you are using Windows, you will need to do the following:
1. Open the Control Panel, and click on **System and Security.**
2. Click on **System.** From the left-hand list, select **Advanced System Settings**. This will open the dialog box shown in Figure 1.4.
3. Click on the **Environment Variables** button, at the bottom of the dialog box. This open another dialog box, shown in Figure 1.5.
4. Click the **New...** button under the System Variables section. This will open the dialog box in Figure 1.6.
5. Enter the variable name **ANDROID,** and set the variable value to the folder where you installed the SDK earlier. Click **OK**.
6. In the System Variables list (after you close the New System Variable dialog box), select **PATH** variable, and click **Edit...** Go to the end of the Variable Value field and enter:

```
;%ANDROID%/tools;%ANDROID%/platform-tools
```

and then press **OK**.

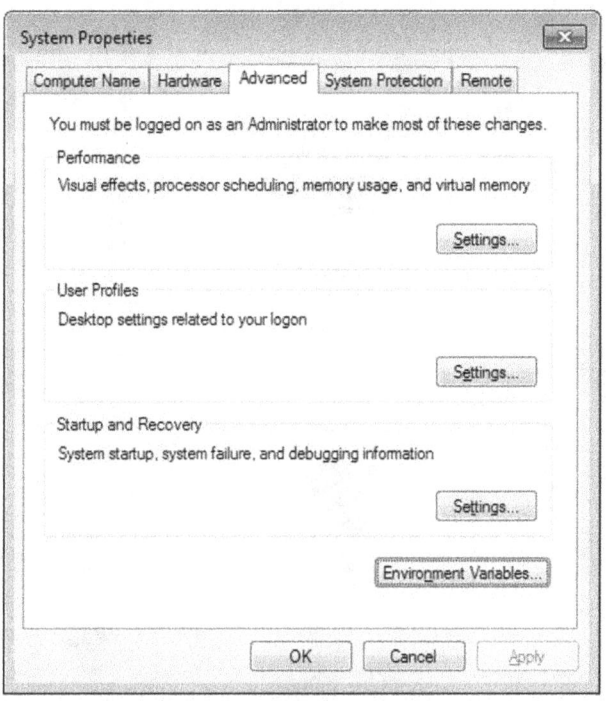

Figure 1.4: The **System Properties** dialog box, open on the **Advanced** tab.

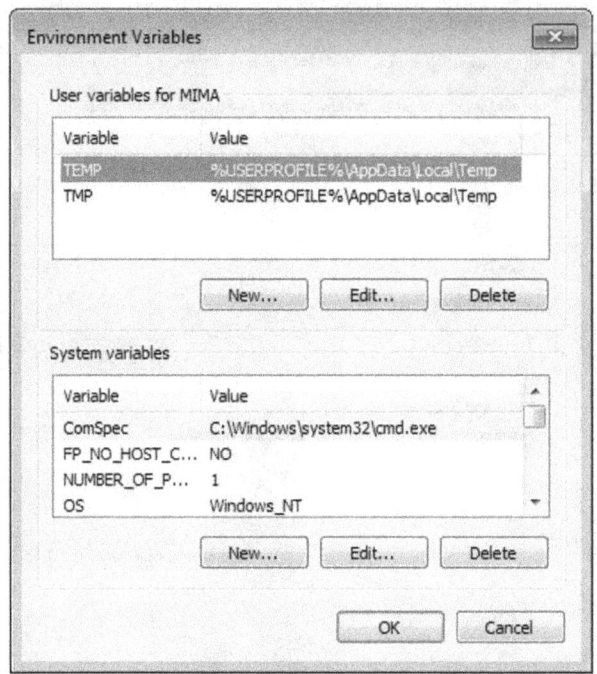

Figure 1.5: The **Environment Variables** dialog box.

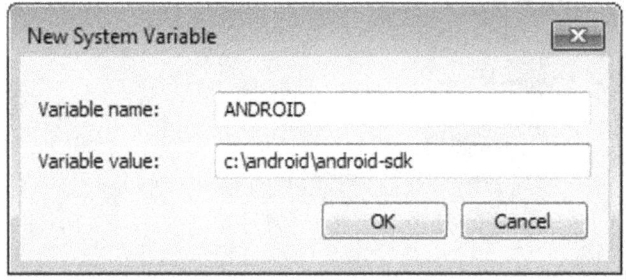

Figure 1.6: The **New System Variable** dialog box.

1.5 Creating a New Android Studio Project

And going back to the Android Studio. After it finishes installing the components we selected earlier, it will open the welcome window, shown in Figure 1.7.

If you are using Windows, you are probably better off installing the Google USB Driver right away. In the same Welcome Screen (as Figure 1.7), click on **Configure**, then select **SDK Manager**. This will open the SDK manager, shown in Figure 1.8.

Figure 1.7: Android Studio Welcome Screen.

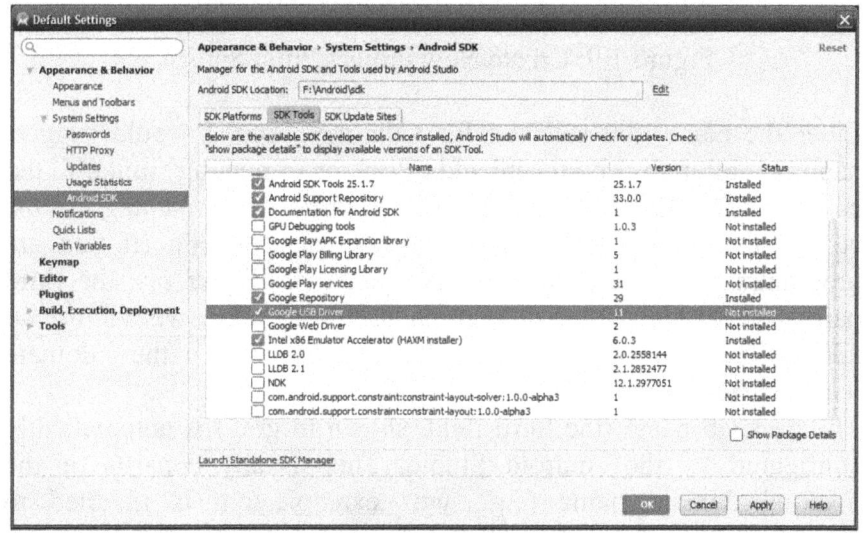

Figure 1.8: The SDK Manager.

Select the **SDK Tools** tab, and scroll down until you find **Google USB Driver**. Check it and click **OK**. You will be prompted to accept the License agreement. Click **Next**. Wait until the component is downloaded and installed, then click **Finish**.

Now, in the welcome screen, select the first item, **Start a New Android Studio Project.** The **Create New Project** window opens (Figure 1.9).

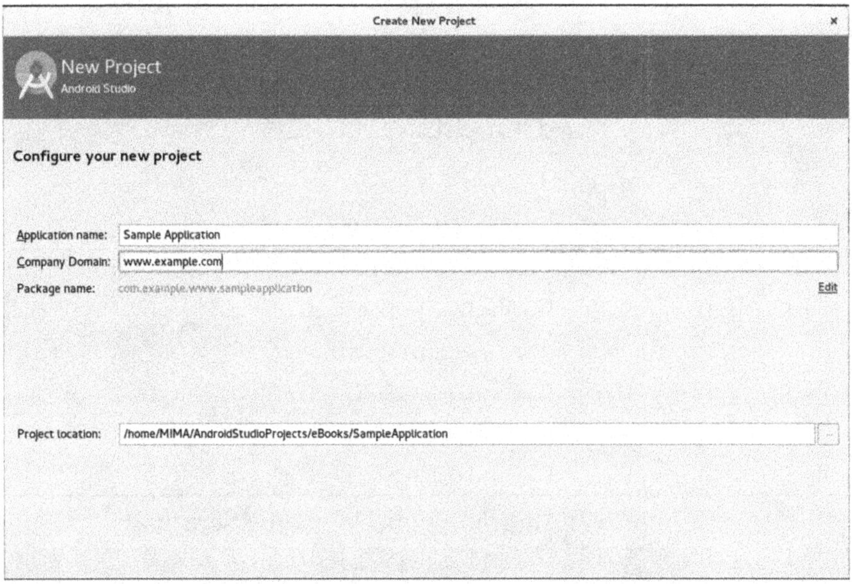

Create New Project	×

New Project
Android Studio

Configure your new project

Application name: `Sample Application`

Company Domain: `www.example.com`

Package name: com.example.www.sampleapplication   Edit

Project location: `/home/MIMA/AndroidStudioProjects/eBooks/SampleApplication`

Figure 1.9: Create New Project: First Screen.

Enter the name you selected for your new App, I would suggest naming it after your book and add eBook or something similar to the end, e.g. *The Killers Novel,* or *The Android Programming eBook*, etc. In the second field, enter the company domain (if you are programming for a third party company, or if you *are* the third party), or use your home domain name. In this book, we will use an application named *Sample Application*, with the domain *www.example.com.*

The package name (the third field, shown in gray) is automatically configured by the Android Studio. This usually consists of the inverted domain name (e.g., www.example.com is inverted to com.example.www, the Top-Level Domain – TLD being first, then the application name is appended to it). This is the full package name that will be used for the application, as Java dictates that its classes be packaged into separate packages this way.

You can select where you want your application files to be saved on the disk by clicking the button with the three dots, to the right of the **Project location** field. After you finish, press ENTER to go to the next screen.

The Android Studio gives you the option to select what type of devices you want your application to run on. The default, **Phone and Tablet**, is already selected. Under this you will find a field labeled **Minimum SDK,** with **API 11: Android 3.0 (Honeycomb),** or perhaps another option, selected from the drop-down list.

The Application Programming Interface (API) is the set of library calls that define how applications interact with the Android system. We will be using those API calls during your App development. With each new version of Android, a new API version is released, newer versions include more features, more library routines and calls, and security and other enhancements.

The Minimum SDK version is a way of telling the Android system the minimum set of API calls that your program needs in order to run. Say, for example, you use an API call that was introduced in Android API 11. If the end user is having API 9 Android 2.3 (Gingerbread), the program will run quietly, until your program tries to access the feature that requires a higher API. At that point, the program will crash, probably throwing a run-time exception, leaving behind a bewildered and angry user who is wondering what on earth happened. The Minimum SDK feature is there to mitigate this particular situation. When the user chooses to install your App from the Google Play Store, the program won't be installed if his API version is below what you stated as the minimum SDK version.

That means, in order to ensure that you cover the largest share of the market, you will try to use the lowest possible SDK version. That doesn't mean you need to use a very low version, as newer versions offer better user (and programmer) experience. In general, targeting API 11 and later will guarantee you covering more than 97% of the market share of Android. You can get more details about the percentage of Android versions running on end devices, along with other useful information, in the Android Dashboards page (https://developer.android.com/about/dashboards/index.html).

The current version of Android is version 6.0, code-named

Marshmallow (API 23). If you noticed, the naming conventions in the Android world are pretty confusing, to say the least. First, there is the Android system version (2.3, 5.1, 6.0, ...). Then, there is the API level. And if that is not enough, there is the code-name. The correlation between the three is well known to Android developers and can be gained with experience, but it is not a mandatory skill. Table 1.1 shows those three categories.

Table 1.1: Correlation between Android version, code-name and API level

Version Name	Code Name	API Level
6.0	Marshmallow	23
5.0 5.1	Lollipop	21 22
4.4	KitKat	19
4.1.x 4.2.x 4.3	Jelly Bean	16 17 18
4.0.3 – 4.0.4	Ice Cream Sandwich	15
2.3.3 – 2.3.7	Gingerbread	10
2.2	Froyo	8

Going back to the **Target Android Devices** window, you do not need to change any thing, just press ENTER.

The next screen, **Add an Activity to Project,** lets you choose the type of Activity you want added to the project. We will talk about Activities in the next Chapter. For now, keep the **Empty Activity** selection and press ENTER. The Android Studio will ask you to name the Activity and the Layout, for which it provided the default values **MainActivity** and **activity_main**, respectively. You will accept both those, leave the **Generate Layout File** checkbox checked, and press ENTER. And voila! Your first Android project is created!.

Chapter 2: The Structure of an Android App

2.1 General Overview

If you have done any sort of programming before, you probably know the difference between an *application* and a *process* (sometimes called a *task*). An application is *static* program code, usually saved on a file system on some storage medium, like a disk drive. A process is *dynamic* program code, residing in memory, actively processing data or doing other functions.

When an Operating System (OS) loads an executable image file from storage media, it copies the image into memory, usually in segments, one for the data and another one for the code. The OS then needs to activate the program by calling a certain *entry point*, usually a function called *main()* in most C-derived programming languages.

The situation is quite different under the Android regime. An Android App doesn't have a designated entry point, the App can essentially be called through any one of multiple entry points, which are called the program's *activities* (more on that in the next section).

Android is an application platform that is built on top of the Linux kernel. That doesn't mean that Android *is* Linux, this is *not* true. Android is built *on top* of Linux, just like my Fedora Linux Workstation is a complete OS built *on top* of the Linux kernel.

But being a Linux-descendant means that Android bears many things from its parent:

- Android, like Linux, is a multi-user, multi-tasking operating system. But unlike a traditional Linux system, where each human (or machine) user can run his own programs, under Android, each App is considered a separate user.

- As in traditional Linux, each user has a unique user ID (UID). In Android, this is also true: each App (thence a user) is assigned a unique UID. This UID is important because it dictates file permissions on the system: no user (thence an App) can access the files belonging to other users, which means no App can modify, update or delete the files belonging to other Apps.

- Each process runs in its own task space (sometimes called virtual machine – VM). This is the process model under Linux, and it ensures no one process can step over the toes of other processes. This is important from a security standpoint, as malware cannot infest other processes to multiply and infect the system. Furthermore, if a process goes down for whatever reason, it is not bound to bring the whole system down with it.

2.2 App Components

An Android App consists of one or more of the four kinds of application components, which are: **activities**, **services**, **content providers**, and **broadcast receivers**. We will discuss them in turn in the next sections.

2.2.1 Activities

An Android activity is a single screen that the user sees on the User Interface (UI). For our purpose, think of the eBook you will build as such: one activity will be the screen showing the Table of Contents, another activity will be the Reading Area where the body text of a chapter is shown, a third activity will be the Search area, and so on.

As activities are the screens the user sees on the UI, **Views** are the building blocks of this interface. A view is part of the visible area that is used to display a specific part of the interface. Some examples are: a **TextView** which is used to show text to the user, an **ImageView** which is used to display images, and a **Button** which is exactly that: a button!.

As we are developing in Java, Activities are implemented as Java classes that are descendants (subclasses) of the **Activity** Java class.

2.2.1.1 Activity Life-cycle

During the life-cycle of an activity, from its creation until its demise, many things happen. The Android system interacts with your activity and gives it chance to do any work that needs to be done, before going to the next step. At any point in time, an activity can be in one of three states:

- *Resumed/Running* state: this is when the activity is in the foreground of the device's screen and is getting user focus and input.
- *Paused* state: this is when the activity is not in the foreground, but it is still visible. This happens when the user opens another activity that covers only part of the screen, or is partially transparent. Your activity is alive at that state, but it doesn't have user's focus.
- *Stopped* state: this is when another activity completely covers yours. Your activity is now in the background, and is not receiving any input from the user.

In the *paused* and *stopped* states, your activity is alive, but the system may kill it later if the device runs down on memory and the system needs to free memory for other, more important, tasks.

During its transition between the three states, an activity is called by the Android system to do whatever is needed to prepare for the coming state. For example, when stopping the activity, the system calls the activity to give it a chance to save the state of the App, in case the user re-opened it later and wanted to start where he stopped before.

Figure 2.1 shows the activity life cycle. It shows the different callback functions that the Android system calls in your activity in turn:

- When the activity is first launched, the Android system calls onCreate(). This function is responsible for initializing the essential components of the activity, and defines the layout for the user interface. This call is followed by a call to onStart().
- onStart() is called just before the activity becomes visible to the user. It is followed by a call to onResume() if the activity is coming to the foreground, or by a call to onStop() if the activity is going to the background.
- onResume() is called after the activity is visible in the foreground, just before it becomes interactive with the user. The activity is running until another activity hides it, or the user navigates away, at which point onPause() is called

(Arrow 1 in Figure 2.1).

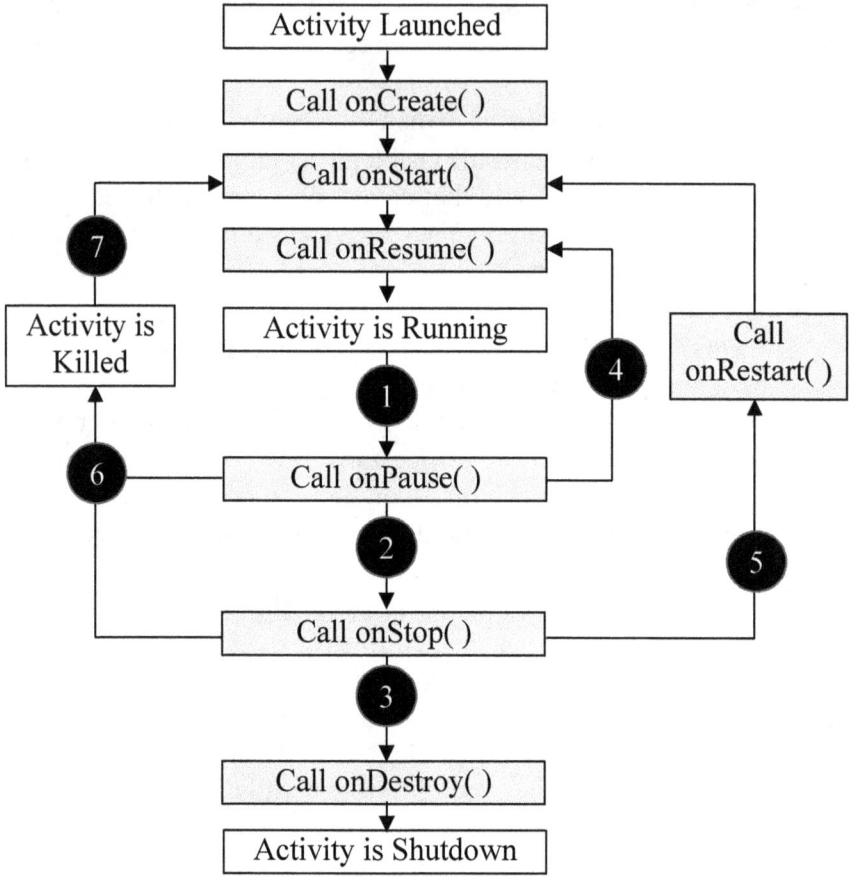

Figure 2.1: The Activity Life-cycle.

- onPause() is called when the system is about to start another activity. This method is used to save app data in case the activity is destroyed later, but it should be quick and short. If the activity is returned to the foreground, onResume() is called (Arrow 4 in Figure 2.1), otherwise onStop() is called (Arrow 2 in Figure 2.1).
- onStop() is called when the activity is not visible to the user, as when another activity is covering the screen

completely. If the activity is being destroyed, a call to `onDestroy()` will follow (Arrow 3 in Figure 2.1). If the activity will come back to the foreground, a call to `onRestart()` will follow (Arrow 5 in Figure 2.1).

- `onDestroy()` is called when the activity is being destroyed, and is the final call the activity receives during its life-cycle.
- `onRestart()` is called after an activity was stopped, before being started again. It follows a call to `onStop()`.

In case the system needed to free memory for higher priority tasks (Arrow 6 in Figure 2.1), it will kill the background activity. If the user later navigated back to the activity (Arrow 7 in Figure 2.1), the system will create a new instance of the activity by calling `onCreate()`.

As such, the activity has three lifetimes, nested inside each other:

- The **entire lifetime** is between the call to `onCreate()` and the call to `onDestroy()`.
- The **visible lifetime** is between the call to `onStart()` and the call to `onStop()`. The activity is on the screen and the user can interact with it.
- The **foreground lifetime** is between the call to `onResume()` and the call to `onPause()`. The activity is in the foreground and is receiving user input.

2.2.2 Services

Sometimes your App needs to do some work in the background, that is, it doesn't need to show the user what is being done in the foreground. This usually is done for long running tasks, like downloading a file over the internet, or playing some music in the background while the user continues his other work. In our specific example, a service might be useful to load chapter text from the book's database, while the user is shown a "Loading.." message or something else to keep him from being bored. As such, the service itself doesn't provide a UI, and another Activity usually needs to call it in order to start its job, while the activity maintains the user interface.

Just as for activities, Services are implemented as Java classes that are descendants (subclasses) of the **Service** Java class.

We are not going to use services in this book. For loading data from the database we will use threads, implemented via the asynchronous task (AsyncTask) class.

2.2.3 Content Providers

As we said above, the Android system shields each App data from other Apps. But still, Apps need to communicate data between each other. This is where content provides fall into the picture. A certain App (A) has some data that another App, (B), needs to access. App (A) will grant read (or write) access to App (B) to the specific data it wants to share, and will provide it to the other App by using a content provider. App (B) can then query App (A)'s content provider to read/write the shared data, by using a special type of object called a **ContentResolver**.

Content Providers are implemented as Java classes that are descendants (subclasses) of the **ContentProvider** Java class. We are not going to use them in this book.

2.2.4 Broadcast Receivers

A broadcast is a system-wide announcement of an event. For example, say the user has turned the screen off. The system *broadcasts* a message to all listening applications to let them know that the screen has been turned off. A video player might use this broadcast to pause its video playing, for example.

Broadcast Receivers are implemented as Java classes that are descendants (subclasses) of the **BroadcastReceiver** Java class. We are not going to use them in this book.

2.3 Intents

As we saw in the previous sections, an Android App is a loosely coupled string of beads, those beads are the different components that form the App. This is unique to the Android system, and its in fact a powerful and useful aspect. Each App has different entry points, through its components. Each component can start any other component. Apps can call components of other Apps to delegate services to them. Your App doesn't have, for example, to implement the camera functionality itself, it can just delegate this job to the builtin camera App who will happily take the picture and return it to your disposal.

But how do components interact? They use a special message system called an **Intent**. Intents are thus asynchronous messages that are delivered between components. You send an intent to tell another component what you want it to do, i.e. what is your *intent* of the communication.

Intents are created as objects of the type *Intent*. We will use them heavily to communicate between the different activities in our app.

An intent can be either **explicit** or **implicit**.

When the user clicks an item in the Table of Contents (TOC) activity, we will send an intent message telling the Reading activity to load the specific chapter and section into view. We are calling a specific activity with a specific mission: this intent is **explicit**.

Now the user is reading the text he selected. Inside the text, we will embed the different tables, figures, and footnotes as hyperlinks. Another activity in our App will handle those hyperlinks and view the requested resource. To pass the information between the Reading activity and the other activity, we can't tell the second activity explicitly what to do (we are embedding the links in HTML mini-documents). In that case, we would send an intent to the system telling it to look for an App that can view our resource. The system will look into its tables and find out that the only App that has this capability is ours, and specifically the Viewing activity of our App. The system will start our App (if not already started) and load the viewing activity, and send it the intent. In this scenario, we didn't tell the system *which* component to load, we only told it *what* action we needed: this intent is **implicit.**

Intents can be used to activate only three of the four types of components, namely: activities, services, and broadcast receivers. Content providers are activated by firing a request through a **ContentResolver** object. We will not go into details, but you can read more about this in the Content Providers developer guide (https://developer.android.com/guide/topics/providers/content-providers.html).

The intent object you will pass to the Android system when you request some action should contain enough information for the system to decide what component to start, along with information (or data) the recipient will need to perform the action. This information includes:

- *Component name:* this is optional. If you include it, you make the intent **explicit**. If you drop it, the intent is **implicit**, the system will use other data from the intent to decide which which component to start. In general, if you are calling a component of your application, use an explicit intent. If you are calling other applications' components, use implicit intents.
- *Action:* a string specifying what action to perform. This piece of information determines what type of data the intent carries. One of the most common actions is ACTION_VIEW, which is used on data that can be "viewed", like a website, a map address or a photo.
- *Data:* the data contained within this intent, on which the recipient would work.
- *Category:* another string giving extra information about who can handle this component.
- *Extras:* a list of key-value pairs of data that are required to perform the specified action.
- *Flags:* extra pieces of meta-data that are mainly of use to the Android system.

2.4 Dissecting the Android Studio Project

Now we will look at the components of the Android Studio we created earlier in Chapter 1.

If you still have that window open, go there and follow the discussion. If you closed it, run the Android Studio, and either select the **Sample Project** (or whatever you named the project earlier) from the left-hand list, or click on **Open an Existing Android Studio Project** item and open the project (this might take a while, be patient).

The Android Studio window is shown in Figure 2.2.

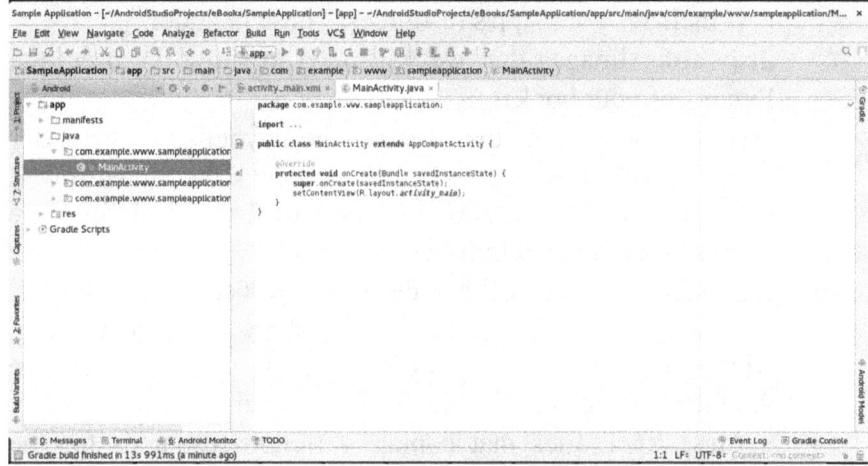

Figure 2.2: The Android Studio Window.

On the left-hand side you see the Project Navigation pane. The top of the tree is **app**, which encompasses all your application files. It contains the following components:

1. **manifests:** click the little arrow to the left of **manifests,** it will show **AndroidManifest.xml**. This is an eXtensible Markup Language (XML) file that tells the Android system about the components of your App. Double click it to open the file (Figure 2.3). It contains important information about the App:

   - The **application** tag defines your App's characteristics: the icon (android:icon), the title (android:label), and the theme (android:theme).

   - The **activity** tag (inside the **application** tag) defines each activity your App has, which the system should know about. If an activity is not listed here, the system doesn't know about its existence, and hence it can't be run.

   - Other components (e.g. services) must be included here to declare them to the system.

2. **java:** click on the little arrow to show the components. Click on the little arrow to the left of the first item (**com.example.www.sampleapplication** in our example) to show the declared Java classes. For now, there is only one class, **MainActivity,** which is the activity we created during the project's creation earlier on.

3. **res:** includes your App's resources. These include:

- **drawable:** Images that we will need to show the user (the Figures of your book).
- **layout:** XML files that define the layout (i.e. the user interface) of different activities. If you click the little arrow, it will reveal one item, **activity_main.xml,** which defines the layout of the MainActivity class.
- **mipmap:** Here we will put the icons we need in our App. If you click the little arrow, it will show **ic_launcher.png,** which is the icon Android system will put as the Application's icon in the Application launcher menu.
- **values:** XML files that contain different resources for the application. We will use the **strings.xml** file in our App later.

4. **Gradle Scripts** (not part of **app**): Files used by the Gradle build system to create your App.

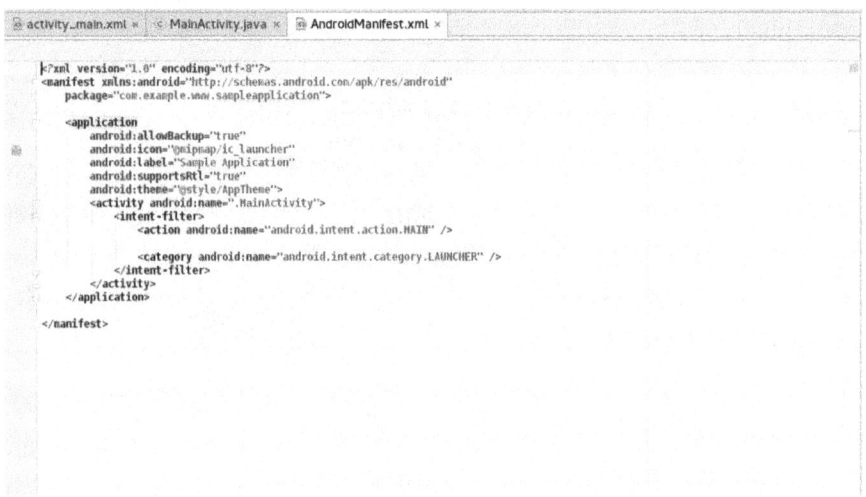

Figure 2.3: The AndroidManifest.xml File.

2.5 Drawable Resources

Open your file explorer (Windows Explorer for Windows, Files for GNOME, Dolphin for KDE) and navigate to the project's directory. Open the **app** (application) folder. Open the **src** (source) folder, then open the **main** folder. Here you will find the **AndroidManifest.xml** file, and two folders: **java,** containing the files for your Java classes;

and **res,** containing the resources. Inside the **res** folder you will find folders corresponding to the different resources in the App: **drawable, layout** and **values.**

But wait a minute, what are the **mipmap-hdpi, mipmap-mdpi, mipmap-xdpi, mipmap-xxdpi,** and **mipmap-xxxdpi** folders?.

It turns out that, in order to run on different device types and screen sizes, Android categorizes screens by defining two characteristics: *screen size* and *screen density.*

The **screen size** defines the physical size of the screen. This can be one of:

- small,
- normal,
- large, and
- x-large.

The **screen density** defines the physical density of pixels on the screen, otherwise known as Dots Per Inch (DPI). This can be one of:

- medium (mdpi),
- high (hdpi),
- extra-high (xdpi),
- extra-extra-high (xxhdpi), and
- extra-extra-extra-high (xxxhdpi).

The system does a pretty good job at resizing drawables to fit different screen sizes. In order to provide the best user experience though, you should include your drawables at different sizes to enhance the look of your application according to the user's screen. Generally, if you include large images, the system can efficiently reduce them to fit into small screens, but the opposite is not true: small images, when stretched, appear pixelated and lose their strength.

You can read more about supporting different screens in the document https://developer.android.com/training/basics/supporting-devices/screens.html.

When we will start making our icons later, we will start with the biggest one, located in the **mipmap-xxxdpi** folder, edit it, and then save it in different sizes in the other **mipmap** folders. An easy way to get the correct icon size is making a copy of the **ic_launcher.png** icon and renaming it, then working on the copy.

Chapter 3: Building the Database

3.1 Why Do We Need a Database?

Well, this is a book we are working with after all, right?. A book mainly consists of text and images (forget about the font format and colors for now). Our App will need to store this data somewhere it can access, in order to view it to the user. For the images, this is simple: use the **drawable** and the **mipmap** folders to save your artwork, which will be automatically included by the Android Studio in your final application package (APK) file.

But what about text?. Many applications save their text in external files, usually located on storage media like the SD card. But there are some questions that arise:

- What happens if the user's device has no SD card capability, or the SD card is removed by the user, temporarily or permanently?.
- What happens if the user deleted our App files, accidentally or on purpose? What if he formatted the SD card? Remember that files on external media are accessible to the user. He can browse those files directly from his device, or plug it using a USB cable to a computer and see everything there is on the card.
- What about other apps or malware? Remember that external media is world-accessible, and hence other apps can read and modify files on it.
- What kind of the file format you are going to use to save this data? Are you going to encrypt it? How about decryption: are you going to use a third party add-on, or will you implement the decryption algorithm in your app?.

As you can see, there is a lot to reflect on if you selected to put your book's data in external files. There is of course the inherent benefit that your app will use less of the device's internal storage space, which tends to be limited, unlike the SD card, which can be changed with a larger capacity one. But does this lone benefit justify all the risks above?.

If you opt to put your data in internal storage, there is a catch: the size is usually limited, and this might defer some users from installing your app. But overall, the benefits are huge: you will evade all the risks listed above, and you can use Android builtin API library calls to access your files.

So, we settled on saving our text data as part of the application's internal storage space. Then why do we need a database?.

First of all, our type of data (that is, text) is a perfect match for a database. Text data is easily saved and retrieved from databases, especially if you are using a lightweight database like SQLite, which is builtin into the Android API library.

The second thing is that the SQLite interface takes all the fuss off your head: how to open a database file, how to query it, how to save and retrieve data, how to update the database, how to search for specific text, and so on.

And lastly, SQLite database files are automatically saved by the Android system in an application designated folder in the internal storage, you don't need to worry about file names and access permissions.

3.2 What Is SQLite?

SQLite (https://www.sqlite.org) is a software library, written in C, to implement a self-contained, server-less database engine. Self-contained means the engine does not need external resources to do its job. Just plug the engine into your platform (as Android, PHP and others do) and there you are: the database engine is ready to go.

Server-less means that, unlike other database systems, it doesn't need to connect to a remote (or even local) server to provide its functionality. All you need is available there in the database file.

SQLite is a public domain software, which means any one can use it, improve it, re-distribute it, and do whatever one likes with it, no fees incurred. The current version of SQLite as of this writing is 3.13.0, and can be downloaded from https://www.sqlite.org/download.html.

If you are running a GNU/Linux box, you probably have SQLite already installed on your system. You can check this by opening a terminal and running:

```
$ sqlite3
```

Which is the SQLite version 3 interpreter. If it is installed, it will show something like:

```
[MIMA@localhost android-studio]$ sqlite3
SQLite version 3.11.0 2016-02-15 17:29:24
Enter ".help" for usage hints.
Connected to a transient in-memory database.
Use ".open FILENAME" to reopen on a persistent
database.
sqlite>
```

You can exit the interpreter by typing (there is a dot in front of **quit**) and pressing ENTER:

```
.quit
```

3.3 Creating Our Database

Database access means we need to speak database language, which is SQL (Structured Query Language) or a subset thereof, like SQLite. But I promised you not to worry about programming, right?. This is why we will need some tools to help us get around the dirty database work without getting our hands soiled (much).

There are many *database editors* that provide a Graphical User Interface (GUI) front-end to SQLite. Those editors will let you do the CRUD operations (Create, Retrieve, Update and Delete) on your database in an easy graphical way: click a button, select an item from a list, and you are done.

One of the good options is the **DB Browser for SQLite** (http://sqlitebrowser.org/). It is a small utility editor, available for GNU/Linux, Windows and Mac OS. You can download it from the website and install it on your system. If you are running GNU/Linux, you probably can get it through your system updater. If you are using an RPM-based system, you can run from a terminal:

```
sudo dnf install sqlitebrowser
```

On older systems, you need to use `yum` instead of `dnf`.

After installing the package, run it from the Applications menu (or Start → All Applications for Windows users). You can also run it from the terminal:

```
sqlitebrowser
```

Either way, the window shown in Figure 3.1 should appear.

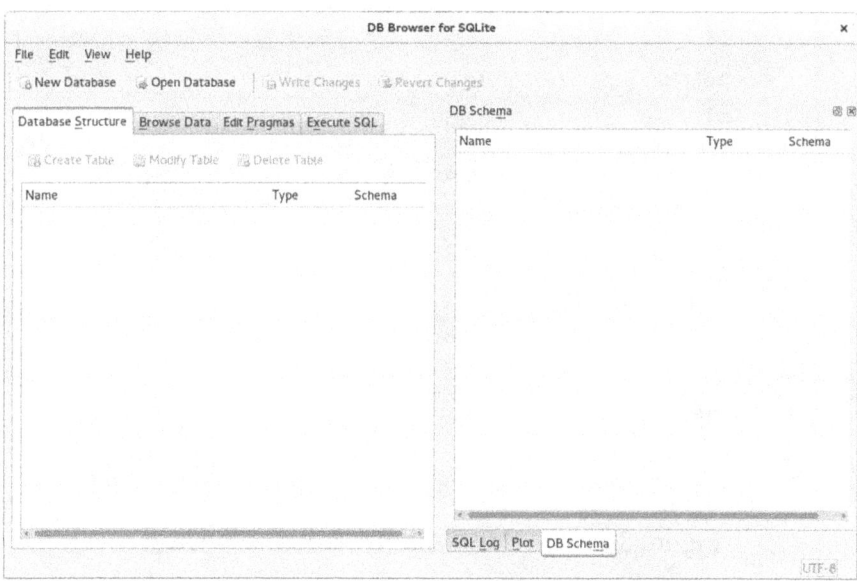

Figure 3.1: DB Browser for SQLite Main Window.

Click on the **New Database** button. It will open a file browser. Navigate to your Android Studio project's directory, and enter **SampleApplicationDB.sqlite** as the file name, and click **Save**. The database file is created, and the **Edit Table Definition** window appears (Figure 3.2).

In the **Table** field, enter a name for the table (I advise giving a name that reflects the book's name, like *book_title_table*). Use underscores instead of spaces to separate the words. In the figure, I entered: *mybook_table*.

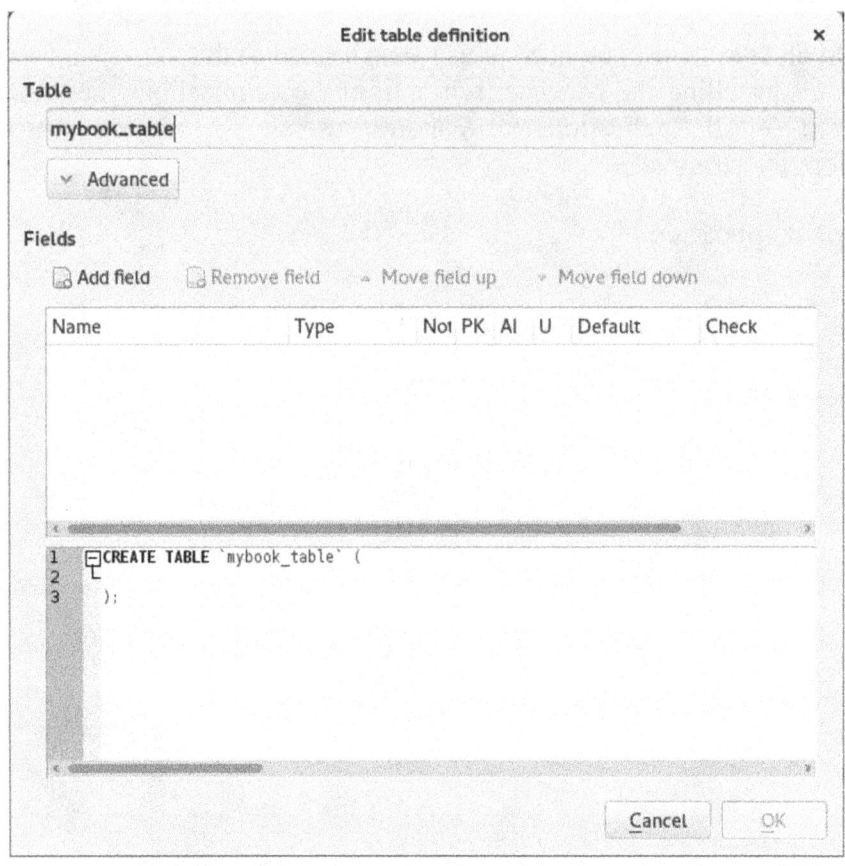

Figure 3.2: The Edit Table Definition Window.

Click the **Add Field** button. Add the following field:
- Name: double click on **Field1** to edit. Enter **Chapter** and press ENTER.
- Type: select **INTEGER** if not already selected.
- Not Null: check the check box.

Click the **Add Field** button again. Add the following field:
- Name: double click on **Field2** to edit. Enter **Section** and press ENTER.
- Type: select **INTEGER** if not already selected.
- Not Null: check the check box.

Click the **Add Field** button again. Add the following field:

- Name: double click on **Field3** to edit. Enter **BodyText** and press ENTER.
- Type: select **TEXT** if not already selected.
- Not Null: check the check box.

Click the **Add Field** button. Add the following field:

- Name: double click on **Field4** to edit. Enter **_id** (with a leading underscore) and press ENTER.
- Type: select **INTEGER** if not already selected.
- PK (Primary key): check the check box.

As you edit the fields, the text field at the bottom shows you the actual SQLite syntax that the editor will use to tell SQLite to create the table in the database. After you finish, click **OK**.

Now the table is shown under the **Database Structure** tab to your left. The **Name** field shows table names, and the **Schema** field shows the structure of the table inside our database.

Now click **Write Changes** from the toolbar to save the new database structure to file. If at any point you think you made a mistake, you can click **Revert Changes** to rollback the database to the state it was in before you made the changes. *Beware though:* this **will not** work after you click the **Write Changes** button!.

After saving your changes, close the browser. Now the database file is ready.

I suggest you open your file browser, navigate to your application's directory, and make a copy of this file. Call it something like **SampleApplication_Clean.sqlite**. This file will become handy in case you made mistakes and corrupted your database while you are practicing.

3.4 Preparing Your Manuscript

You most probably created your manuscript in the first place using a word processor like Office Word, LibreOffice Writer, or Mac Pages. Those word processors are good, but in our case, they are an overkill.

In order for the word processor to apply all the formats, colors, figures, shapes, and everything else you used to create your outstanding manuscript, it needs to include meta-data in the file you save. So, for example, if your file is called **manuscript.docx,** this file includes headers, formatting meta-data, and much overhead that we don't need. What we need is to save our files as plain text files. What we will do to the manuscript includes the following:

- Create a new folder under your App's directory, call it **dbprep** (short for Database Preparation). This is where all the following files will be saved.
- If you have the manuscript in one file, you will need to separate each chapter in a separate file. Put all the introduction, including the preface, acknowledgments, and everything up to (but excluding) chapter 1 in one file. Remove the Table of Contents; Lists of figure, List of tables List of and side-boxes from the file. This will be chapter 0 (zero).
- Every subsequent chapter will be having sequential numbers, starting at chap1, chap2, and so on, until the end of text.
- If you already have your manuscript separated in files, just make sure you follow the above naming and numbering system, and copy all the files to the **dbprep** folder your created in the first step.

Next, we will convert those files into plain text files. But before we do that, we need to stop for a minute and take a breath.

What we are about to do is to convert each chapter into a plain text file. We could take all the text and save it into one cell in our database's table, but this is not efficient.

We assume that most users will view our eBook in medium-to-small device screens, such as those of phones and tablets. It is not in our best interests to provide large chunks of data at once. For one, this will greatly reduce the application's speed as it will need to access the database every time it loads a new chapter. The user will not benefit anyway from this large amount of data due to the screen constraints.

What we will do is that we will divide each chapter into sections. Think about each heading as a section, provided there is some text between this heading and the next one. In order to do this, we will need to insert some instructions into each file, to demarcate sections start and end positions, where tables and figure are, and some other information.

The next step is to run those files through a utility program I wrote specifically for this purpose. The program will read each file in turn, parse it to read the instructions, and formulate the SQLite commands that we will feed to the **DB Browser for SQLite** in order to put our book in the database.

The utility I wrote can be downloaded from:
http://sites.google.com/site/mohammedisam2000/android-app-ebook/dbprep.

The source code (one C file, over 1300 lines) can be obtained from:
http://sites.google.com/site/mohammedisam2000/android-app-ebook/dbprep.c.

If you downloaded the source file, you can compile it to an executable using the **gcc** (GNU Compiler Collection) which is installed by default on GNU/Linux boxes. Open a terminal, navigate to where you downloaded the source file, and invoke:

```
gcc -o dbprep dbprep.c
```

The -o option tells gcc the output file name, which is **dbprep** in this case. If you don't provide this, gcc will write the executable to a default file named **a.out**.

If everything goes well, the gcc will not give you any feedback. You can check that the executable is created by running:

```
ls -l
```

Which will show you both the C source file and the executable (shown in bold).

```
[MIMA@localhost dbprep]$ ls -l
total 172
-rw-r-----. 1 MIMA MIMA 22838 Jul  4 23:09 chap1.txt
-rwxrwx---. 1 MIMA MIMA 37824 Jul  8 09:57 dbprep
-rw-r--r--. 1  MIMA  MIMA  34034  Jul  5  00:12
dbprep_BKUP.c
-rw-r--r--. 1 MIMA MIMA 41324 Jul  8 09:57 dbprep.c
```

```
-rwxrwx---. 1 MIMA MIMA 13648 Jul  8 08:43 fixfigs
-rw-r--r--. 1 MIMA MIMA  3493 Jul  8 08:43 fixfigs.c
drwxr-xr-x. 2 MIMA MIMA  4096 Jul  8 09:36 in
drwx------. 2 MIMA MIMA  4096 Jul  8 09:57 output
[MIMA@localhost dbprep]$
```

If you downloaded the executable directly from my website, it would probably not have it's executable bit set. To do so, you need to enter in a terminal:

```
chmod +x dbprep
```

then

```
ls -l
```

to check that the executable bit is set.

3.4.1 Understanding dbprep's Instructions

The **dbprep** utility needs instructions to know what to do exactly. In the same directory you were in, open a plain text editor (like NotePad on Windows or GEdit on Linux) and write the following lines:

```
PackageName="com.example.www.sampleapplication"
Table=mybook_table
Chapter=""
Final=SectionHead
Separator=SectionEnd
SectionHead=""

InsertTable=""
Separator=
Final=EndTable

InsertBox=""
Final=EndBox

InsertFigure=""
```

On line 9, the one that reads: "Separator=   ", there is a hidden tab after the equal sign. Be sure to insert it.

Save the file as **orders.txt** in the **dbprep** directory you created earlier.

Those are all the instructions you will need to insert into your files to make them **dbprep**-readable. The instructions are:

- *PackageName:* this tells **dbprep** what is the package name that you entered when you created your Android Studio Project in the previous chapters.

- *Table:* this is the name of the table that you created in **DB Browser for SQLite** earlier.

- *Chapter:* this will contain the name of the chapter as it appears in the Table of Contents.

- *Final=SectionHead:* this tells **dbprep** where the sections start. In this case, they start right after the keyword **SectionHead** is encountered.

- *Separator=SectionEnd:* tells **dbprep** where the sections end. In this case, they end right before the keyword **SectionEnd** is encountered.

The above five instructions occur once per each file, at the very beginning of the file. The next instructions appear as much as needed throughout your files:

- *SectionHead:* this tells **dbprep** where each section starts, and provides the name of the respective section, as it appears in the Table of Contents. The text of the section follows, starting from the next line after this one. Everything is section's text until we encounter the **SectionEnd** instruction. This will be repeated for each section in every chapter.

- *InsertTable:* when there is a table in the text, you will surround it with **InsertTable** and **EndTable** instructions, so that **dbprep** will know where the table starts and ends. In order for **dbprep** to know what separates the columns (usually a single tab or a comma), the **Separator** instruction tells it that. Notice that in the above list there is a tab character after the "Separator=" keyword which is not shown in the print.

- *Final=EndTable:* tells **dbprep** what phrase marks the end of the table body. In this case, whenever **EndTable** is encountered, that means the table has ended.
- *InsertBox:* the same as InsertTable above, to insert a side-box. The box's body text extends until an EndBox instruction (or whatever is specified in the "Final=" instruction that follows) is encountered.
- *InsertFigure:* tells **dbprep** that a figure is to be inserted in that place. Between the quotes you will insert the name of the *file* that holds the figure, not the figure *title*. You will need to incorporate the title within the figure itself. There are some restrictions on file naming, which we will discuss later.
- *InsertFootnote:* tells **dbprep** to insert a link to a footnote. The text between the quotes is the text that will appear to the user as the link. Everything that follows is the body of the footnote proper, until the next newline character. That is, a footnote can span only a single line, however long it is.

This is the vocabulary of **dbprep**'s language. We saved these in a file in the **dbprep** directory so that you can come back to it whenever you needed a refresher, and you *will*.

3.4.2 An Example on Using dbprep

This **dbprep** stuff is probably overwhelming for you, right?. We better off have a little practice before delving deep into your real book files.

Open your file explorer, navigate to the **dbprep** directory, and create a new folder named **test.**

For this exercise you will need to open a simple text editor. My favorite ones are GEdit and Kate for GNU/Linux (you can use NotePad for Windows). Whatever your text editor is, open it and enter the following lines:

```
PackageName="com.example.www.sampleapplication"
Table=mybook_table
```

```
Chapter="Introduction and Preface"
Final=SectionHead
Separator=SectionEnd
SectionHead="Introduction"

This is the introduction of my book.
It goes on and on.

SectionEnd
SectionHead="Preface"

This book is very important and you will need to read
it to understand how important it is.

SectionEnd
```

Save this file as **chap0.txt** in the **dbprep/test** folder you made above. Close this file.

Create a new empty file (CTRL+N usually does the trick). Insert these lines (you can copy and paste them if you feel lazy and this is an electronic version of this book!):

```
PackageName="com.example.www.sampleapplication"
Table=mybook_table
Chapter="Chapter 1: The First Chapter"
Final=SectionHead
Separator=SectionEnd
SectionHead="1.1 Introduction to Chapter 1"

Here we speak about the importance of having a first
chapter in a book.

SectionEnd
SectionHead="1.2 What comes next?"

And then we go on and on about what's next.
And here is a table to show it.

InsertTable="Table 1.1: What's next"
Separator=
Final=EndTable
```

```
First Column      Second Column
#1      ..
#2      ..
EndTable

SectionEnd
SectionHead="1.3 The One With the Box"

This is a section with a box.

InsertBox="Box 1.1: Just an Example"
Final=EndBox
Here comes the body of the box.
EndBox

SectionEnd
SectionHead="1.4 Final Section"

Have a look at Figure 1.1.

InsertFigure="Figure1.1"

This      figure      is,        according        to
InsertFootnote="WikiPedia"
Check it out at www.wikipedia.org
, an awesome one!.

SectionEnd
```

Save this file as **chap1.txt** in the **dbprep/test** folder you made above.

Notice that in the "Separator=   " line, right after "InsertTable=...", there is a TAB character right after the equals sign. Don't put any empty lines between InsertTable and EndTable.

Close this file. Open a terminal and change directory to the **dbprep** folder, where you have the **dbprep** program. Now enter:

```
./dbprep test
```

You invoke the local program, named **dbprep** (hence the "./", as the local path is not part of the executable path in GNU/Linux for security reasons), and you passed it a folder name, **test** in this case.

The **dbprep** utility creates a folder named **output** by default. If you want to change this behavior, just invoke it with the name of the input folder, followed by the name of the output folder, such as:

```
./dbprep test output-folder
```

Note that you cannot specify an output folder and skip the input folder, i.e. if you pass only one folder to the utility, it will assume that it is the input folder.

If you just invoke the utility with no arguments at all, i.e.:

```
./dbprep
```

It will assume the input folder is the current working directory (or "."), and the output folder is a subfolder herein by the name of **output**.

Now run the program as we said, passing it only the **test** folder as an argument. The output in your terminal should look like (lines are rounded up due to the page size):

```
[MIMA@localhost dbprep]$ ./dbprep test
>>>>>>>>> Parsing: chap0.txt <<<<<<<<<
chap0.txt: Found 0 table(s), 0 figure(s), 0 box(es),
0 footnote(s) in section 1
chap0.txt: Found 0 table(s), 0 figure(s), 0 box(es),
0 footnote(s) in section 2
>>>>>>>>> Parsing: chap1.txt <<<<<<<<<
chap1.txt: Found 0 table(s), 0 figure(s), 0 box(es),
0 footnote(s) in section 1
chap1.txt: Found 1 table(s), 0 figure(s), 0 box(es),
0 footnote(s) in section 2
chap1.txt: Adding table '"Table 1.1: What's next"': 3
row(s), 2 col(s)
chap1.txt: Found 0 table(s), 0 figure(s), 1 box(es),
0 footnote(s) in section 3
chap1.txt: Adding box '"Box 1.1: Just an Example"'
```

```
chap1.txt: Found 0 table(s), 1 figure(s), 0 box(es),
1 footnote(s) in section 4
chap1.txt: Adding Figure '"Figure1.1"'
chap1.txt: Fixed fig name to '"figure1_1"'
chap1.txt: Adding footnote '"WikiPedia"'
========================
Output written to output/
Fixing the TOC..
Removing temporary files..
Finished!
[MIMA@localhost dbprep]$
```

As you can see from the output, the utility parses the files one by one, inspecting them section by section. The output shows you the details of each section: how many tables, figures, side-boxes, and footnotes are found in each section.

It also shows you the details of each table as it parses it: how many rows and columns are found in each. Notice that the rows count includes the header of the table, so you should expect it to be 1 more than the actual rows count.

3.4.3 Figure Naming Rules

Now look at the following lines from the previous section:

```
chap1.txt: Adding Figure '"Figure1.1"'
chap1.txt: Fixed fig name to '"figure1_1"'
```

If you remember, I told you before that there are restrictions on figure file names. As we are going to add our figures as image files under the **res/drawable** folder, we need to follow those restrictions if we want Android Studio to read them in and include them in our project. The rules are very simple, that is, figure names should consist of the following characters only:

- Small letters a-z,
- Numbers 0-9,
- Underscores.

This, of course, is excluding the dot that marks the end of the name and the beginning of the file's extension.

48

So, in our example, the figure would have been saved as something like "**Figure1.1.png**", and the **InsertFigure** instruction refers to this file, excluding the file extension of course.

Now, as the figure's name doesn't conform to these restrictions (there is a capital letter, and there is a dot), the **dbprep** utility recognizes it and changes it to fit the template. You would save yourself a lot of pain in the back if you named your figure files properly, to start with. A simple scheme of FigureX.X.png (or any other format) would be sufficient to get you going. Try to avoid spaces, special characters, punctuation (including the dot, except in the file extension of course) in the file names. If you need to separate words, do this with an underscore instead of a space.

3.4.4 The output Folder

Now open your file explorer and navigate to the **dbprep** folder. Now you will find a new folder, named **output**, that was created by the utility in the last section. You can also view it by running ls -l (from the **dbprep** folder):

```
[MIMA@localhost dbprep]$ ls -l
total 48
-rwxrwx---. 1 MIMA MIMA 37824 Jul  9 21:25 dbprep
drwx------. 2 MIMA MIMA  4096 Jul  9 21:33 output
drwxr-xr-x. 2 MIMA MIMA  4096 Jul  9 21:33 test
[MIMA@localhost dbprep]$
```

You can look at the contents of the folder by entering ls -l output/:

```
[MIMA@localhost dbprep]$ ls -l output/
total 28
-rw-rw----.  1  MIMA  MIMA   179  Jul   9  21:33
out.boxes.txt
-rw-rw----.  1  MIMA  MIMA   334  Jul   9  21:33
out.chap0.txt
-rw-rw----.  1  MIMA  MIMA   997  Jul   9  21:33
out.chap1.txt
-rw-rw----.  1  MIMA  MIMA    12  Jul   9  21:33
out.figures.txt
```

```
-rw-rw----. 1 MIMA  MIMA      190 Jul    9 21:33
out.footnotes.txt
-rw-rw----. 1 MIMA  MIMA      185 Jul    9 21:33
out.tables.txt
-rw-rw----. 1 MIMA MIMA 1108 Jul  9 21:33 strings.xml
[MIMA@localhost dbprep]$
```

Those are the files created by **dbprep** in the output folder:

- `out.chap0.txt` and `out.chap1.txt`: Every chapter file that the utility reads, it parses and produces a matching output file. Those are the files that we will feed to **DB Browser for SQLite** to construct the database.
- `strings.xml`: If you remember section "2.4 Dissecting the Android Studio Project", we talked about App resources, and mentioned a few of them, including String resources, found in a `strings.xml` file. What we will do later is that we will replace the original `strings.xml` file in the project directory with the one created here by the **dbprep** utility.
- `out.tables.txt`: This contains the tables of all the chapters. We will feed this file later to **DB Browser for SQLite** to add your tables to the database.
- `out.footnotes.txt` and `out.boxes.txt`: Those contain the footnotes and the side-boxes of all the chapters. We will feed those two files later to **DB Browser for SQLite** to add your footnotes and side-boxes to the database.
- `out.figures.txt`: This file contains a list of all the figure names, not as listed in your file, but as they are referred to in the output of the utility. For example, look at the file in your terminal by invoking `cat output/out.figures.txt`:

```
[MIMA@localhost          dbprep]$          cat
output/out.figures.txt
"figure1_1"
[MIMA@localhost dbprep]$
```

Which shows you **Figure1.1** as **figure1_1**, which is the *fixed* name that we talked about earlier.

3.4.5 Adding the output Files to the Database

Now open the **DB Browser for SQLite**. Click on **Open Database** in the toolbar. Navigate to your project directory and open **SampleApplicationDB.sqlite** (or whatever you called the file). Click on the **Execute SQL** tab. It would show you Figure 3.3.

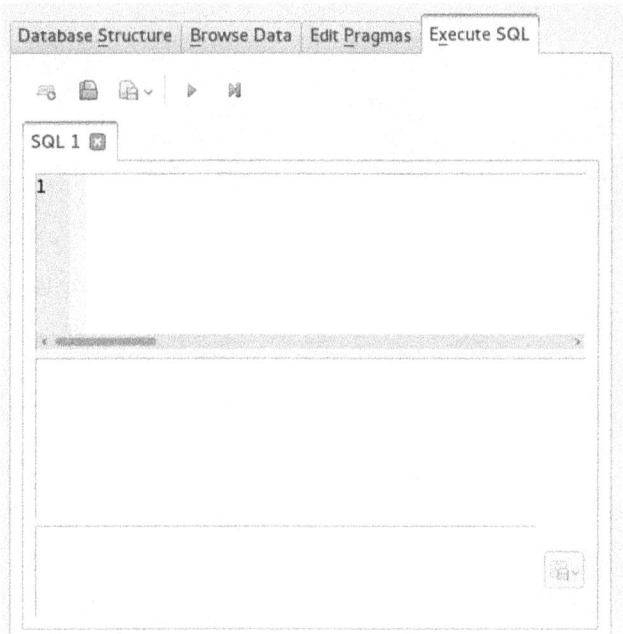

Figure 3.3: The Execute SQL Tab.

Click on the second button from the left (if you hover the mouse on it, it will show "Open SQL file"). Open the **dbprep/output/out.chap0.txt** file. The window will show as Figure 3.4.

You see that the browser has read through the file, recognized the SQL instructions in it, and added them to a list. If you are observant, you will notice that **dbprep** has appended the tag "**
**" to the end of each line of the text. This is important as we will display the text as HTML text later. HTML doesn't recognize the newline character at the end of lines, so we have to tell it where exactly the line breaks are (hence "br", for break). You don't need to do this manually,

dbprep does it for you when it reads your chapter files.

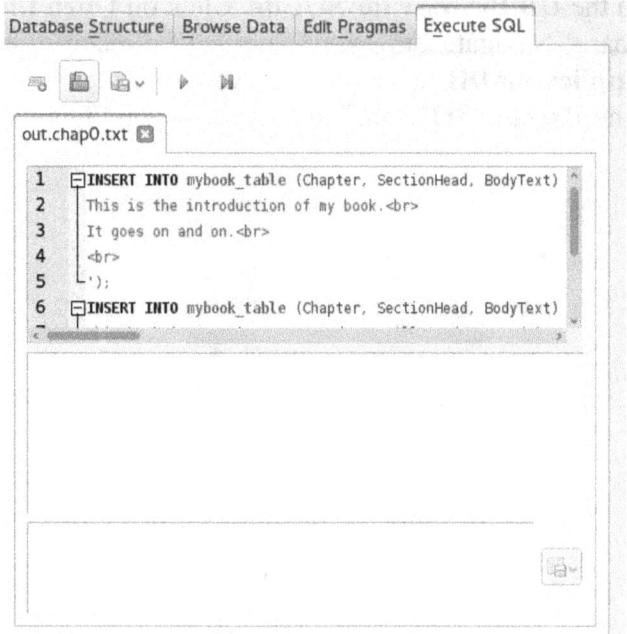

Figure 3.4: The **out.chap0.txt** File Open.

Now click the second button from the right, with the blue arrow (if you hover the mouse over it, it will show "Execute SQL [F5, Ctrl+Return]"). You can also press F5, or CTRL+ENTER to call it. The browser tries to execute the SQL instructions in the file. But the output (in the text area at the bottom) reads:

```
table mybook_table has no column named SectionHead:
INSERT INTO mybook_table (Chapter, SectionHead,
BodyText) VALUES (0, 0, '
This is the introduction of my book.
It goes on and on.

');
```

What happened?. Well, when we created the table earlier on, we added a field named "Section". But in fact, **dbprep** expects it to be named "SectionHead". We will remedy this now.

Go back to the **Database Structure** tab, click on the table (I named it **mybook_table**, use yours if you named it differently). Now the **Modify Table** and **Delete Table** buttons are enabled. Click on **Modify Table**, which will open the window in Figure 3.5.

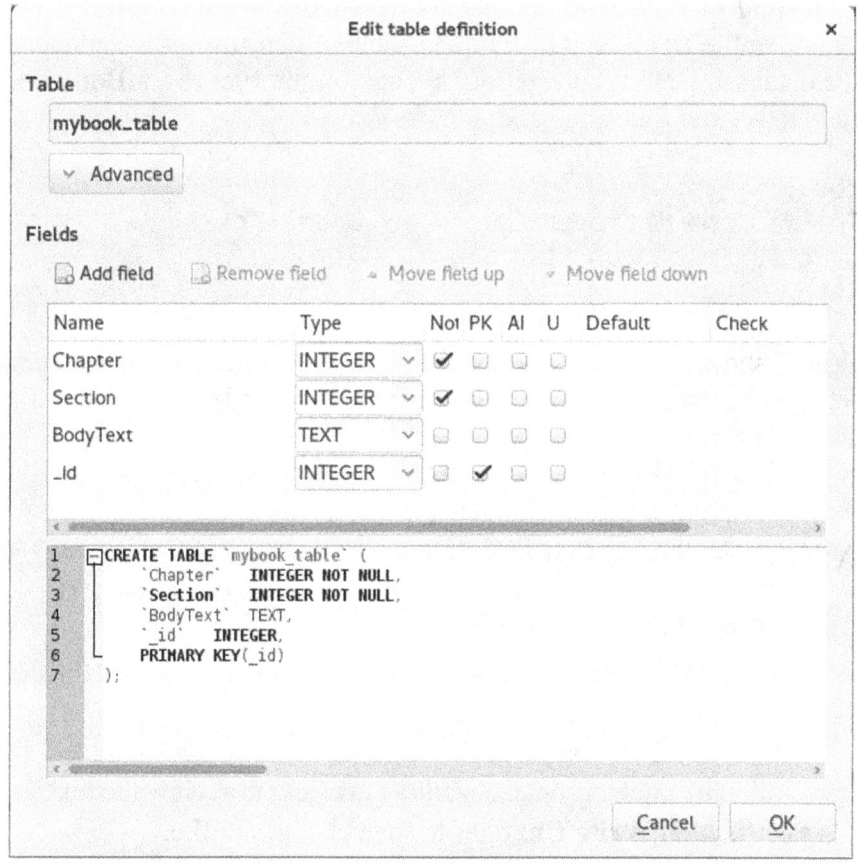

Figure 3.5: The **Edit Table Definition** Window.

In the fields list, double click on **Section** and type **SectionHead**, then press ENTER. The SQL command for table creation changes accordingly. Click **OK**.

Now click on **Write Changes** to write the new database structure to file. Now would be a good time to replace the copy we made of the database file with a new copy, reflecting the correct database structure.

Now go back to the **Execute SQL** tab and click on the **Execute SQL** button. This time, the output area shows:

```
not an error:
```

Indicating that the SQL commands were executed successfully. You can open the **Browse Data** tab and see that two rows were added to the database table. You can double click on the first row's **BodyText** field to see the following text:

```
<br>
This is the introduction of my book.<br>
It goes on and on.<br>
<br>
```

Which shows the body text of the first section in our introduction (chapter 0), with the **
** tags appropriately added to indicate the ends of lines.

Now click on **Write Changes** button to write the new table to file. Now repeat the same for Chapter 1:

- Open the **Execute SQL** tab.
- Click on **Open SQL File** button, and open **out.chap1.txt**.
- Click on **Execute SQL** button.
- The SQL commands are executed successfully, as indicated by the "not an error:" output.
- Go to the **Browse Data** tab and review the text we added, by double clicking on each **BodyText** field to review the text.
- Click on **Write Changes** to save changes to file.

Now do the same with the files: out.boxes.txt, out.tables.txt, and out.footnotes.txt in turn, to add the side-boxes, tables and footnotes to the database. Remember to click **Write Changes** to make changes permanent.

Now go back to the **Browse Data** tab. Open the **Table** drop-down list. You will find 4 tables listed:

- *Boxes:* this contains the body text of all the side-boxes in your book.
- *Footnotes:* this contains the body text of all the footnotes in

your book.

- *mybook_table:* this contains the body text of your book proper, except that for the tables, footnotes and side-boxes.
- *table0:* this is the first table ever found in the book. Later tables would be named table1, table2 and so on.

Open each table in turn to review its contents. It is always a good idea to review your changes before clicking the **Write Changes** button to commit changes permanently to the database.

Now close the database browser window, and open your file browser. Navigate to your project's folder. Open the **app** folder, then open the **src** folder, then open the **main** folder. You should see two folders: **java** and **res**, and one file: **AndroidManifest.xml**. Create a new folder and name it **assets**. Assets are extra resources your App needs. You will now copy the database file (*SampleApplicationDB.sqlite*) from the main project's folder to the **assets** folder you just created, so that Android Studio can see it.

Now open the Android Studio and open your project. Look in the Project Navigation pane to the left. Between **java** and **res**, you should see a new item called **assets**. Click the small arrow to the left of **assets**, you should now see the database file, *SampleApplicationDB.sqlite*, listed there.

3.5 Doing It in the Real World

We will continue our work in this book using the sample application and the sample chapter files we just created. But I will show you how to work with your real chapter files so that you can apply what you learned on your real eBook project.

I will demonstrate this by using a sample document, which I show you in Figure 3.6. You can use your book's introduction or a short chapter from it to follow through. Make sure the chapter you selected contains at least one table.

If you didn't do it yet, you need to open your book manuscript and divide it into separate chapter files. You can do this by selecting a whole chapter, then opening a new document, pasting the copied chapter, and then saving the new file with an appropriate name, e.g. **chap1.docx** (remember that **chap0.docx** is reserved for the introduction and preliminary material).

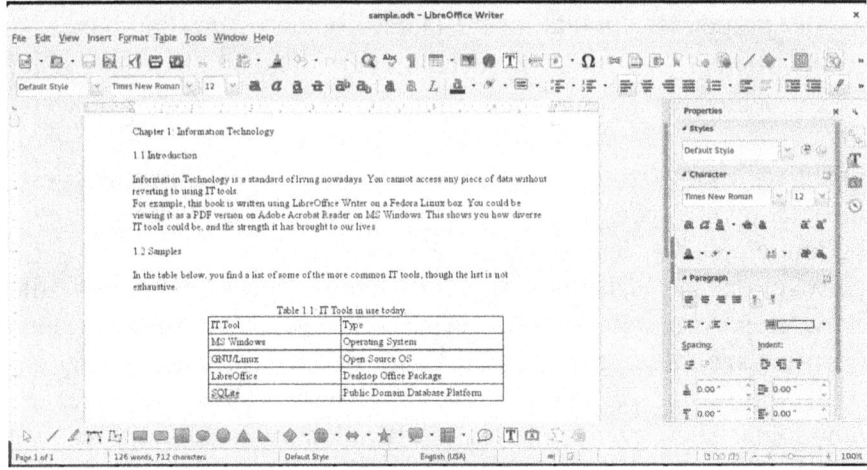

Figure 3.6: Sample Toy Document.

I am using LibreOffice Writer for this demonstration. You are free to use Office Word or Mac Pages, or whatever you word processor is, just follow the instructions and apply them to your word processor as appropriate.

Now open the **orders.txt** file (we created that earlier in section "3.4.1 Understanding dbprep's Instructions"). Copy the first 6 lines (Down to the line that says SectionHead="""") and paste them **first thing in your file,** that is, those lines *must* be at the head of the file, before *anything* else.

Cut the chapter name (**"Chapter 1: Information Technology"** in our toy document) and paste it between the quotes in the third line, right after "Chapter=".

Cut the header of the first section ("1.1 Introduction" in our toy document) and paste it between the quotes in the sixth line, right after "SectionHead=".

Scroll down to the end of the first section. Insert a new line and add "SectionEnd" as one word with no spaces (and without the quotes).

Right after the last line with "SectionEnd", insert a new line and add "SectionHead=" (without the quotes). Add the title of the second section between two braces in this line. Close this section with a

"SectionEnd" instruction at the end (without the quotes), right before the next section begins.

The overall document now should look similar to Figure 3.7.

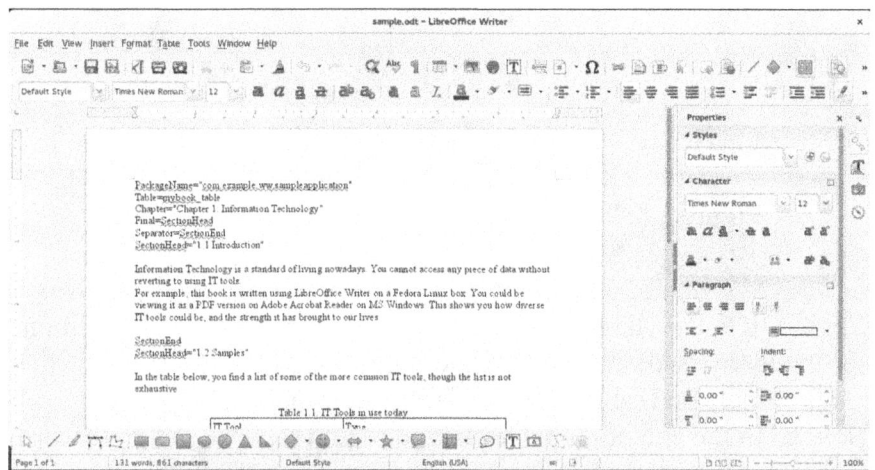

Figure 3.7: The Partially-edited Toy Document.

Now, we need to deconstruct your tables to make them dbprep-friendly.

Copy lines 8-10 from your **orders.txt** file, which read:

```
InsertTable=""
Separator=
Final=EndTable
```

Remember that the "Separator=" line contains a TAB which is not shown in the print. Make sure the tab is there by clicking on the line, then pressing the END key. The caret should go far beyond the equals sign, where the non-printed TAB ends. This is **important,** as **dbprep** expects you will tell it what separates the columns of any table.

Select the first table in your document, and paste those three lines right before the table. Cut the table's name and paste it between the quotes, right after "InsertTable=".

Click anywhere inside the table. In LibreOffice Writer, open the **Table** menu, and select **Convert → Table to Text**. This opens the dialog box shown in Figure 3.8.

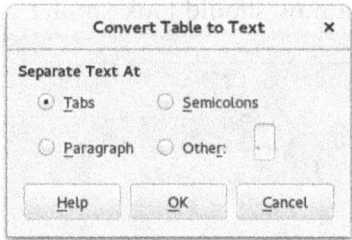

Figure 3.8: The **Convert Table to Text** Dialog Box.

Click OK. The table is now converted to text, with columns separated by TABs. Delete any empty lines between the line that reads "Final=EndTable" and the first row of the table.

Now go to the end of the table, and add "EndTable" as a single word, with no spaces, and without the quotes, on a separate line. Make sure there are no empty lines between the final row of the table and this line. The final look should be like Figure 3.9.

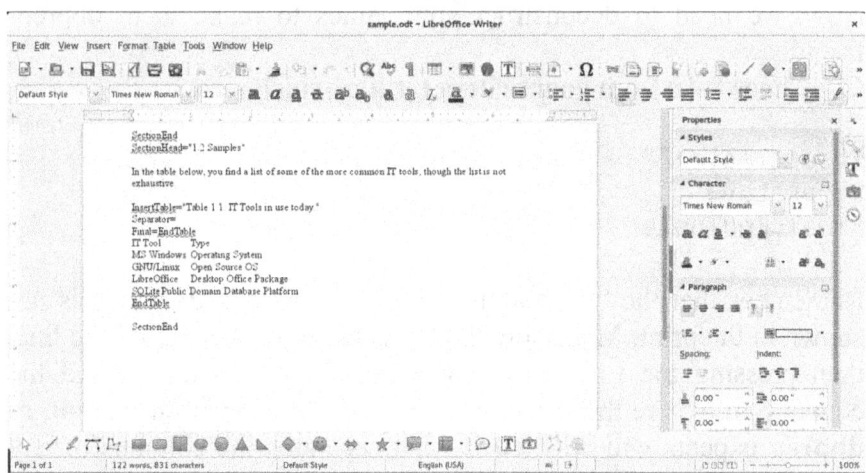

Figure 3.9: The Toy Document With Deconstructed Table.

If, for any reason, you needed your table columns to be separated by any character different that TAB (say, for example, there are cells with tabs inside of them), you will need to replace the TAB after

"Separator=" with the other character you are using.

Finish editing your chapter by adding "SectionEnd" and "SectionHead=" at the end and the beginning of each section, respectively. Any figure you encounter, you need to remove it and put in its place a line that reads:

```
InsertFigure=""
```

Insert the respective figure file name between the quotes, e.g. Figure1.1, and so on.
Any side-boxes (if you use them) must be encased between

```
InsertBox=""
Final=EndBox
```

before the side-box (put the box's title between the quotes), and

```
EndBox
```

after the side-box.
Any footnotes should be replace by

```
InsertFootnote=""
```

with the text you want displayed as the link to the footnote between the quotes. The footnote text proper should follow on the next line. If your footnote spans multiple lines, you will need to remove that and make the footnote fit into one line, however long it would be.

Now you need to save your chapter as a plain text file. Under LibreOffice Writer, open **File** → **Save As...** (or press CTRL+SHIFT+S). The **Save As...** dialog box opens. In the **Name:** field, append **.txt** to the file name, so that **chap1** would read **chap1.txt**, and so on.
If you are using Office Word, you need to open **Save As** from the **Office Button**, and select "Plain Text (*.txt)" from the **Save As Type** drop-down list at the bottom of the dialog box.
Now close the file, and reopen it. It should show you the text in an

ugly monospaced font. This is because all the meta-data for formatting are removed from the file, you are now working with a raw text file which contains *only* text.

One final note before we go: all quotes must be simple quotes which looks like ("). If you see any quotes in the text file that look like (") or ("), you need to replace them with the above looking quote. You can do this by selecting **Edit → Find and Replace** (or pressing CTRL+H in both LibreOffice Writer and Office Word) and clicking **Replace All**.

Now create a folder named **in** under your **dbprep** folder (we created this inside of the project's directory before). Copy all the plain text files (**chap0.txt, chap1.txt, ...**) into this folder. Remove the **output** subfolder if it exists, and invoke from a terminal:

```
./dbprep in
```

If the output shows "Finished!" in the last line, and the output folder shows files that look like: **out.chap0.txt., out.chap1.txt,** ... that correspond to your chapters, along with the tables, figures, footnotes and boxes files, then everything has went just fine.

Now open the **DB Browser for SQLite**, open your database file, and follow the steps in section "3.4.5 Adding the output Files to the Database", to create your book's database.

3.6 I Have Equations In My Book

If you have equations in your manuscript, those will need some extra work.

Equations are a special type of object. They are handled differently between the different word processors, and they won't fit properly as raw text.

One workaround is to format your equations as HTML text.

You will need a WYSIWYG (What You See Is What You Get) HTML editor. A good one is called **KompoZer** (get it from http://kompozer.net/download.php). It works under Windows, GNU/Linux and Mac OS. Download and install the program, then run it. The window looks like Figure 3.10.

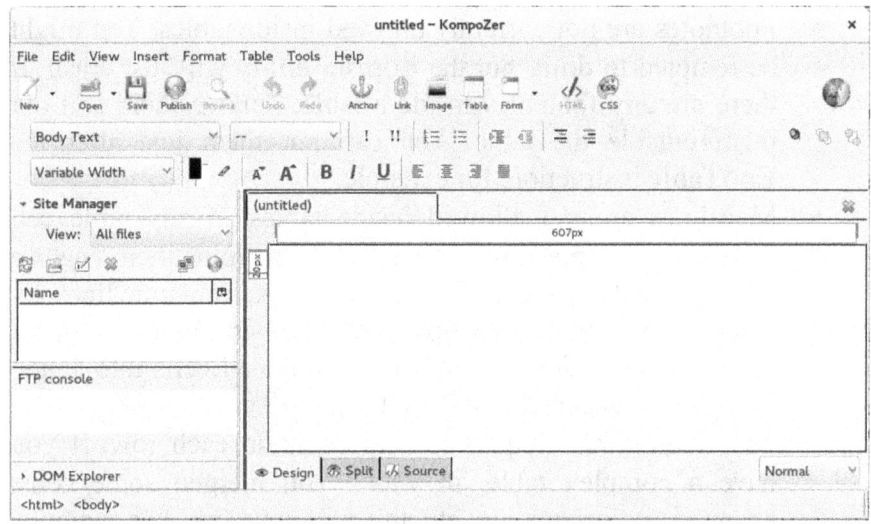

Figure 3.10: KompoZer Window.

Enter your equation in the *Design* area. Use **Format → Text Style** from the menu to add effects to your text, e.g. adding super- and subscripts, bold face, etc.

When you are satisfied with the looks of your equation, switch to the *Source* tab. Select everything that lies between the **<body>** and **</body>** tags and copy it. Go back to your word processor and paste this in place of your equation. It looks ugly and cryptic, but it should show quite fine when you view it in your App later.

3.7 Final Notes Before You Go

Those are some tips that will help you formatting your manuscript correctly in order for the **dbprep** utility to produce correct SQL output files:

- No text is allowed outside a section. For example, some books include preliminary material after each chapter's head, right before the first section. This will not work. You need to include this preliminary material in a section. Call it **Section 0** or **Preliminary Section** or **Chapter Introduction,** the choice is yours; but remember: *no text* is allowed outside **SectionHead** and **SectionEnd** instructions.

61

- Footnotes are not currently allowed inside tables. You might be tempted to do it, but the **dbprep** utility will just crash. If there are any footnotes inside a table, remove them and out them outside the table. You can put them just after the **EndTable** instruction, for example.

- Multilines are not allowed inside tables. If any table cell contains multiple lines, you need to join them *before* converting the table into plain text. You can join lines by inserting commas, full-stops, spaces, or any other character of your choice. Just remember to reduce all cells into single lines *before* deconstructing the table.

- Tables must have equal column count in each row. If you have a complex table, in which you merged some cells, changed text orientation, etc, this will not work. For example, if the maximal column count is 5, it must be 5 in all rows of the table. Pad the rows with less columns using empty cells at the end of the row to make them equal.

- What you put inside the quotes after "InsertFigure=" is the **file name** of the figure, not the **title** of the figure. The title of the figure has to be included in the figure file, as part of the figure itself.

- If you have a numbered list, you need to remove the automatic numbering and add the numbers manually as regular text.

- If you have a bullet-list, you need to remove this and add a manual list indicators, like a star (*) or a dash (-) in front of the list items.

- Quotes must be simple quotes like ("), not (") or (").

- If you have a Table of Contents (TOC) in your introduction, remove it. **dbprep** will dynamically create a new TOC whether you want it or not.

- If you have a separate List of Tables, List of Figures, or List of Side-boxes, remove them all. **dbprep** will dynamically create them all.

I know these look like an awful lot of restrictions, I will try to eliminate those restrictions in future versions of **dbprep**. Meanwhile, think of them as a small price you have to pay to get your eBook

App developed in the fastest and easiest way possible.

Sometimes you will have figures that are not images, but objects you constructed inside your word processor. Those will need to be converted into plain images in order to be added to the App. You can do this in several ways:

- The easiest way is to open your file and center the figure in view. You can then press the **PrtScr** (Print Screen) button on your keyboard (usually located at the upper-right corner, near the Caps-Lock LED indicator). Under GNU/Linux, this will result in a screenshot saved to your Pictures folder, in a file named **"Screenshot from DATE TIME.png"** (where DATE and TIME are numbers corresponding to the date and time the screenshot was taken). You can open this picture with **Shotwell Viewer**, which will allow you to crop it, removing the surrounding window and keeping only the figure proper. Press CTRL+S to save your changes and close the program.

- If you are using KDE desktop, you can use the **KSnapshot** program to take a screenshot. This is handy because it gives you the option to take a screenshot of the entire screen, of a certain window, or a region of the screen you select manually.

- If you are using GNOME, there is the **Screenshot** utility that does a similar job to **Ksnapshot**.

- Another way that is harder, but one that gives you more control over the process, is to copy the objects from LibreOffice Writer, open a new document in LibreOffice Draw, and paste the objects there. You can edit, move, and do whatever you need to the objects, and save them in an Open Document Format Drawing (ODF Drawing), which has the extension **.ODG**. This file can be edited later if, for example, you are writing a new version of your book. You can export the drawing from LibreOffice Draw by selecting **File → Export As Images...** (If you can't find it on your File menu, it's probably because the plugin is not installed by default. You will need to download it from http://extensions.libreoffice.org/extension-center/export-as-images

and follow the instructions in
http://www.libreoffice.org/assets/Uploads/EN_Documents/Installingextensions.pdf
to install it on your LibreOffice).

Chapter 4: Adding the Main Menu

4.1 Creating an Android Virtual Device

When developing for Android, you will need to test your project as you go to make sure what you wrote in code actually works in the real world. You have two options for testing: using an Android Virtual Device (AVD), or using a real physical device (like your actual phone).

We will start using an AVD. Open Android Studio if not already open. Open the AVD Manager by clicking on the button denoted "AVD Manager" in the toolbar, as shown in Figure 4.1.

Figure 4.1: The AVD Manager Button on the Android Studio Toolbar.

This will open the AVD Manager's window, shown in Figure 4.2 (the list in your fresh installation will be empty, unlike what is shown in the figure).

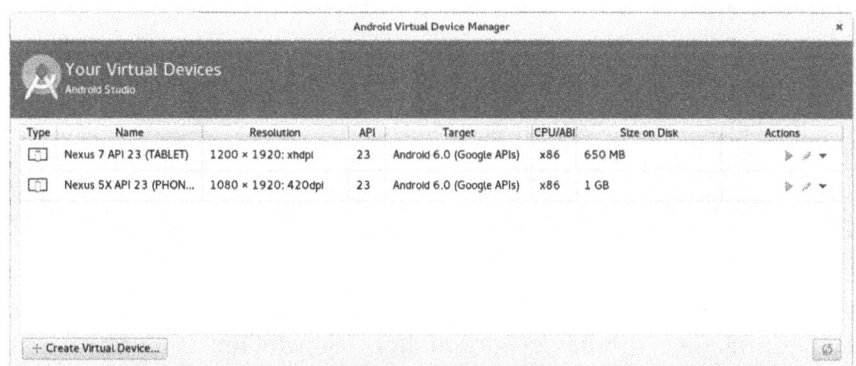

Figure 4.2: The Android Virtual Device Manager Window.

Click on the **Create Virtual Device...** button in the bottom-left corner. This will open the Virtual Device Configuration window (Figure 4.3).

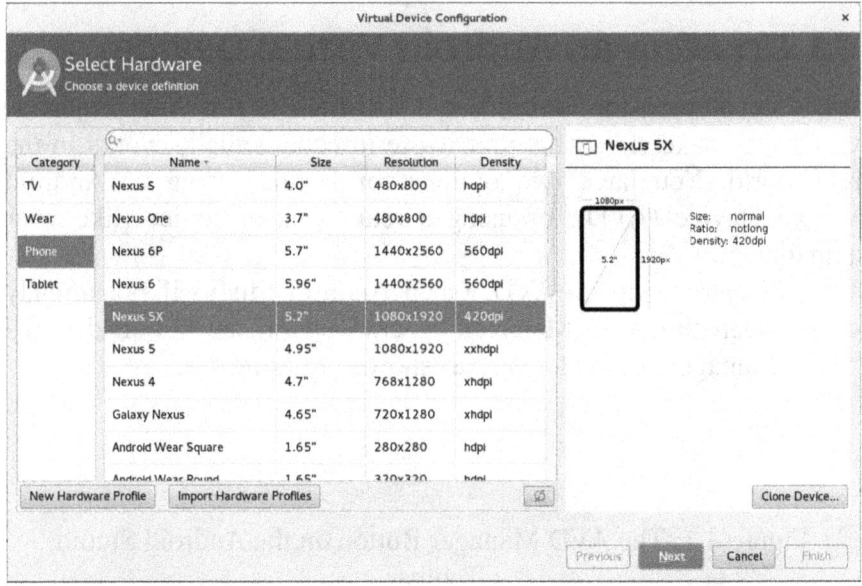

Figure 4.3: The Virtual Device Configuration Window.

Select **Phone** from the left-hand list if not already selected. Select **Nexus 5X** (the fifth item in the middle list) and click **Next**.

In the **Recommended** tab, under **Release Name**, select **Marshmallow** (the first one, with **ABI** x86). There is a blue **Download** link to the right of **Marshmallow**, click on it. Wait for the image to download (you will need an Internet connection for this to work) and install, then click **Finish**.

Back in the Virtual Device Configuration window, select the image you just downloaded, then click **Next**. The final window (Figure 4.4) will show.

You can edit the AVD name if you find the default one unsettling. You can change the device orientation (the default is Portrait, you can choose Landscape). Click **Finish**. The AVD Manager window will refresh to show the newly added device. Close the Android Device Manager window.

Figure 4.4: The **Verify Configuration** Window.

4.2 Testing the Sample Application on AVD

Now in the Android Studio, select from the menu: **Run → Run 'app'**. You can also click the green play button on the toolbar, or press Shift+F10. This will open the **Select Deployment Target** window, shown in Figure 4.5.

Under **Available Emulators**, select the AVD you just added and click **OK**.

If the AVD didn't run, giving you a message that tells the device or resource is busy (Figure 4.6), you probably have another virtual machine running. For example, I have Windows XP installed as a guest machine under my GNU/Linux box. I am using Oracle VM VirtualBox as the virtual machine manager. When I have the Windows machine running, the AVD manager gives me this error. I have to close the virtual machine in order to start the AVD.

If everything goes right, the AVD starts, and you see your sample app, with a text showing the famous "Hello World!" message (Figure 4.7). You got your first Android App up and running!.

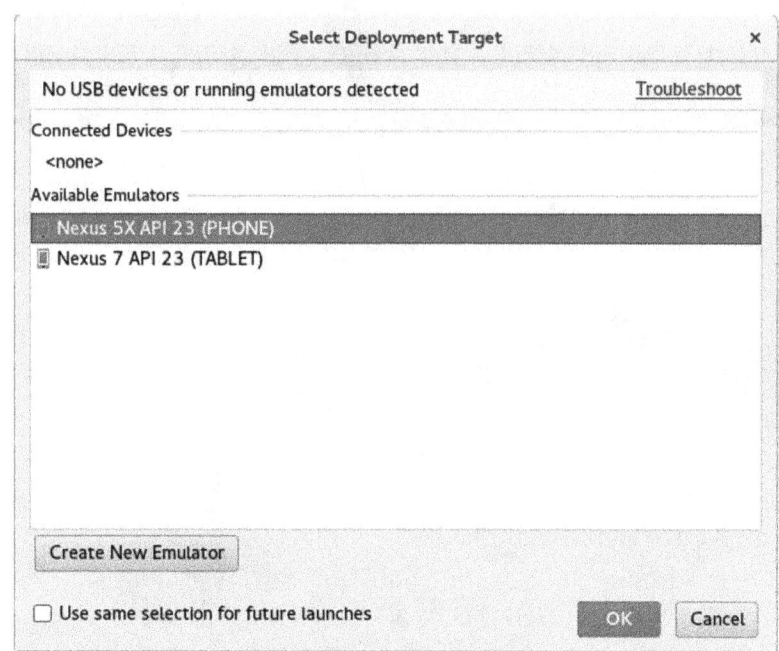

Figure 4.5: The **Select Deployment Target** Window.

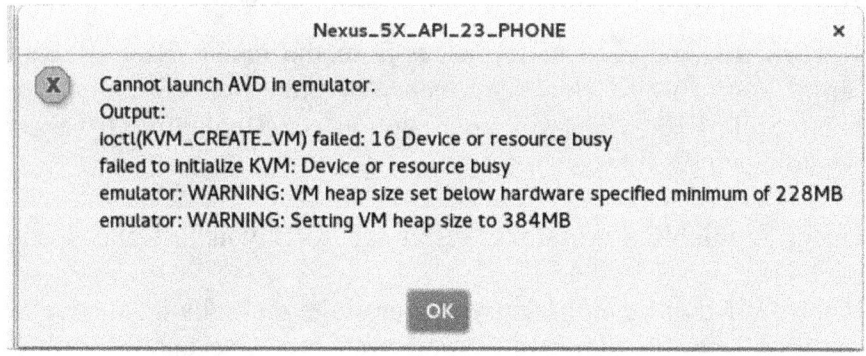

Figure 4.6: Cannot Launch AVD in Emulator Message.

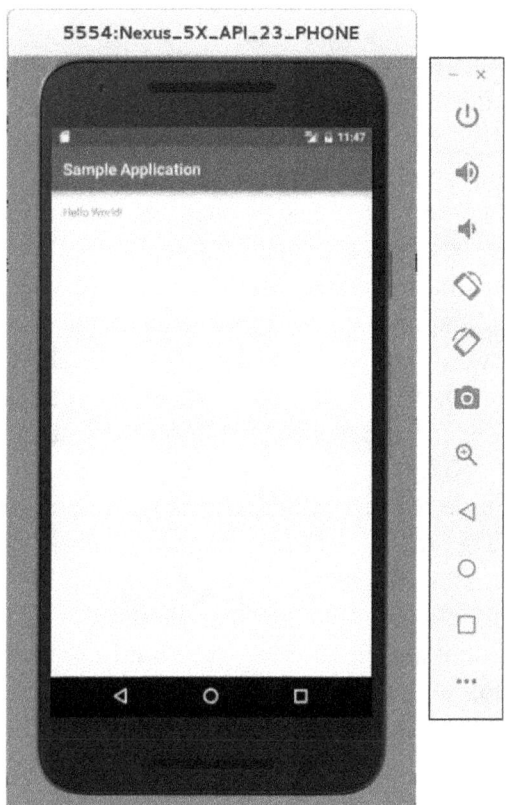

Figure 4.7: The SampleApplication Running in the AVD.

4.3 Creating the MainMenuFragment Class

Remember what we said in Chapter 2 about the activity being a single screen of user interface, and the layout of views within an activity?. Here we have a single activity, the main activity, represented in the MainActivity Java class.

We will need to use something else to implement our main menu. This thing is called a *fragment*.

A fragment is simply a "partial view" of the device's screen. Let's forget about our book here and think about an eMagazine application, that has two parts: news/articles headlines, and the articles themselves.

First, when the user opens the App, it shows the headlines list. This would be implemented as a Java class, say we named it

HeadlinesActivity.

When the user clicks on a headline in the list, it sends an **explicit intent** to the Android system, telling it to launch the other activity, say we named it ReadingActivity, telling it the headline of the requested article, which it is requested to show.

Now we have two activities, one of each can be viewed at any single point in time on the user's screen.

This is fine for small screens, like phones. But what if the user is viewing our application on a larger screen, say a tablet?. One activity would be a waste of space, as the screen would take much more, for example, we can show the headlines list on the left, taking one third of the screen size, and the reading area on the right, taking two thirds of the screen.

But only one single activity can be displayed at one time. So what is the solution?. The solution is in using *fragments*. A fragment is a partial activity. You can create a single activity and add to it any number of fragments to create the final display.

In the eMagazine example above, we would create two fragments, one for the headlines and one for reading, and add them both to the MainActivity. In that way, the user will have both the headlines list and the article he is currently viewing in the same window.

And now, let's get back to our App. In the Project Navigation pane on the left, select the first item under **java** (in our example, it reads: *com.example.www.sampleapplication*). Right click on it, and select **New → Java Class**. In the **Create New Class** dialog (Figure 4.8), enter the following:

- Name: **MainMenuFragment**
- Kind: **Class**

And press **OK**. You can see the new class added below the **MainActivity** class in the Project Navigation pane, and the Java class file is open on the right.

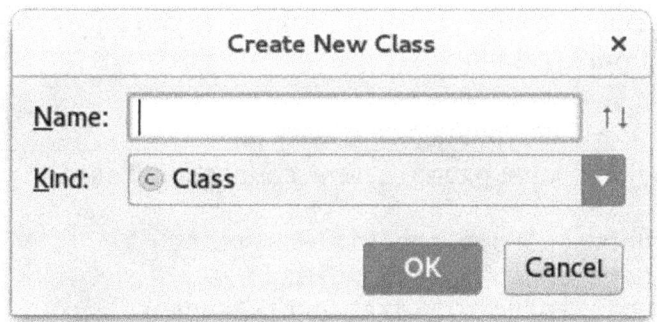

Figure 4.8: The **Create New Class** Dialog.

This class is an empty, simple class. We need to make it a subclass of ListFragment, which is a fragment that displays a list of items. So, in the editor pane on the right, position the cursor just after the word MainMenuFragment, and enter:

```
extends ListFragment
```

the result should look like:

```
public class MainMenuFragment extends ListFragment {
}
```

Notice that, while you are writing, Android Studio gives you options through its code completion feature. When you start writing "ext" it will give you a suggestion to write "extends". You can press Enter to let the Studio insert that word for you. When you start writing ListFragment, it will show you a list of possible completions. You can press the Up and Down keys to navigate the list, and press ENTER to accept the selection. This feature will be very handy when you start writing code.

If you are stuck at any point and need some suggestions, you can press CTRL+Space and the Studio will show you a list of possible suggestions. You can press ENTER to add any of them to the current position you are at.

Now we need to flesh out this class. Position the cursor at the end of the line after the opening curly brace, press ENTER to open a new line, and enter the code shown in Listing 4.1 (you only need to enter the lines from line 14 to 55).

Listing 4.1: MainMenuFragment.java Class Code

```
1     package com.example.www.sampleapplication;
2
3     import android.app.ListFragment;
4     import android.os.Bundle;
5     import android.widget.ArrayAdapter;
6
7     import java.util.ArrayList;
8     import java.util.Arrays;
9
10    /**
11     * Created by MIMA on 7/10/16.
12     */
13    public class MainMenuFragment extends
      ListFragment {
14        private ArrayAdapter<String> listAdapter;
15        public static final int MAIN_MENU = 1;
16        public static final int SUB_MENU  = 2;
17        public static final int LIST_SUB_MENU  = 3;
18        public int whoAmI = MAIN_MENU;
19        public int menuIndex = 0;
20        private String PackageName;
21        private static final int LIST_OF_TABLES = 1;
22        private static final int LIST_OF_FIGURES =
      2;
23        private static final int LIST_OF_BOXES = 3;
24        private static final String TAG =
      "MainMenuFragment";
25
26        @Override
27        public void onActivityCreated(Bundle
      savedInstanceState) {
28
      super.onActivityCreated(savedInstanceState);
29            PackageName =
      getActivity().getApplicationContext().getPackage
      Name();
30            String[] str;
31            if(this.whoAmI == MAIN_MENU) {
```

```
32              str =
    getResources().getStringArray(R.array.toc_main);
33          } else if(this.whoAmI == LIST_SUB_MENU)
    {
34              str = loadList(this.menuIndex);
35          } else {
36              String sub_menu = "toc_" +
    Integer.toString(this.menuIndex);
37              str =
    getResources().getStringArray(getResources().get
    Identifier(sub_menu,
38                      "array", PackageName));
39          }
40          ArrayList<String> menu_items = new
    ArrayList<String>(Arrays.asList(str));
41          listAdapter = new
    ArrayAdapter<String>(getActivity(),
    android.R.layout.simple_list_item_1,
    menu_items);
42          setListAdapter(listAdapter);
43      }
44
45      public String[] loadList(int whichList) {
46          String[] list;
47          if(whichList == LIST_OF_TABLES) {
48              list =
    getResources().getStringArray(R.array.list_of_ta
    bles);
49          } else if(whichList == LIST_OF_FIGURES)
    {
50              list =
    getResources().getStringArray(R.array.list_of_fi
    gures);
51          } else if(whichList == LIST_OF_BOXES) {
52              list =
    getResources().getStringArray(R.array.list_of_bo
    xes);
53          } else list = null;
54          return list;
55      }
56  }
```

If you copied and pasted the code, the Studio would notice that some Java classes are needed by your class, but their containing packages are not imported, so it will suggest doing this for you (Figure 4.9). Press **OK**. Some lines starting with "import" will be added to the head of the file.

Figure 4.9: **Select Classes to Import** Dialog.

Here is what the code in Listing 4.1 does:

- Line 14: This declares an ArrayAdapter class that we will need to display our menu items on the list.
- Lines 15-17: These are constants that will help us know what part of the Table of Contents we are viewing at any point: are we showing the main TOC? Or a list of chapter 1 subheadings? Or the list of tables? etc.
- Line 18: this integer variable will tell us who are we, i.e. what part of the TOC we are showing.
- Line 19: this integer variable will hold the index of the menu item selected by the user. This information will become handy later on.

74

- Line 20: this string variable will hold the package name (currently *com.example.www.sampleapplication*).
- Lines 21-23: if the menu is currently showing one of the three lists (list of tables, figures or boxes) this variable tells us which.
- Line 24: this tag is required by the debugger. It is not mandatory for your program, but we include it because I will show you how to print debug messages in the debugger.
- Line 27: this function, `onActivityCreated()`, is the function Android calls when creating the fragment, right after the call to the activity's `onCreate()` method comes back. In this function we will add the items we need to the list to be displayed to the user as the main menu.
- Line 28: we call the parent's `onActivityCreated()`, to do any necessary start-up.
- Line 29: we get the package name from the application. It is a good idea to get the package name this way instead of hard-coding it everywhere you need to get that name.
- Line 30: declares a string array that we will use to fetch the items of the menu we will display.
- Line 31: tests to see if the menu we are displaying now is the main menu.
- Line 32: if this is the main menu, get the main TOC, which is stored as a string array in the **strings.xml** file (under **res/values**). **dbprep** created this file earlier when it parsed our chapter files, but we haven't copied the file from **dbprep** directory to the **res/values** directory yet. As the TOC is not there yet, the Android Studio shows a red wavy line under **MainMenuFragment.java** tab, and **R.array.toc_main** is shown in red color. We will soon remedy this.
- Line 33: tests to see if the menu we are displaying now is one of the three lists: list of tables, figures or boxes.
- Line 34: if it is so, we call another function, `loadList()`, to load the required list. We will define this function later.
- Line 35: if this is not the main menu and not a list menu, it means we are viewing the TOC of one of the chapters.
- Line 36: the TOC of each chapter is stored in the **strings.xml**

file as a group of array lists, each one is named toc_0, toc_1, and so on until the last chapter. We create a variable, **sub_menu**, which holds the name of the array list we need.

- Lines 37-38: here we fetch the TOC of the current chapter from application's resources.
- Line 40: we create an ArrayList out of the string array we fetched in the previous lines.
- Line 41: we create a ListAdapter and fill it with the ArrayList created in Line 40.
- line 42: we set the ListAdapter we created in Line 41 to be the adapter of the current MainMenuFragment list (remember this class is a descendant of ListFragment). That means whatever is contained in the list, it will be shown on the menu as a list of items.
- Line 45: here we define a function, loadList(), which receives a single parameter, telling it what list we need to view: list of tables, figures, or boxes?. It returns the required list in the form of a string array, String [].
- Line 46: the list we will return to the caller.
- Line 47: checks if the required list is the List of Tables.
- Line 48: if so, it gets the string array named **list_of_tables** from the **strings.xml** file. Again, **R.array.list_of_tables** is shown in red color. We will soon correct this.
- Line 49: checks if the required list is the List of Figures.
- Line 50: if so, it gets the string array named **list_of_figures** from the **strings.xml** file. Again, **R.array.list_of_figures** is shown in red color. We will soon correct this.
- Line 51: checks if the required list is the List of Boxes.
- Line 52: if so, it gets the string array named **list_of_boxes** from the **strings.xml** file. Again, **R.array.list_of_boxes** is shown in red color. We will soon correct this.
- Line 53: otherwise, the call was wrong, and we will return an empty (NULL) list.
- Line 54: return the list to the caller.

Now we need to correct that **strings.xml** situation. Open your file browser and navigate to the project's directory. Open the

dbprep/output folder. Copy the **strings.xml** file. Go back to the project's directory. Open **app** → **src** → **main** → **res** → **values**. Paste the file. You will be asked whether you want to replace the existing file, click Yes.

Now go back to the Android Studio. Double click on the **strings.xml** file in the Project Navigation pane. It will open up the file on the right side. Locate the cursor at the end of the first line (the one that reads: **<resources>**). Press ENTER to open a new line, and enter this:

```
<string name="app_name">Sample Application</string>
```

This string resource was automatically defined by Android Studio in the old **strings.xml** file, the one we replaced above. Without it, the App can never run, as the Studio needs this resource.

Now, if you go back to view **MainMenuFragment.java**, you will find all the red wavy lines and the red words are gone.

4.4 Getting to Know the Layout Viewer

Before we fix the MainActivity class, we need to add something to the layout.

In the Project Navigation pane on the left, double click on **res** to open it. Then double click on **layout** to open it. Then double click on **activity_main.xml** to open it in the right pane.

There are two ways to view a layout: *Design* and *Text* (Item #1 in Figure 4.10).

The *Design view* shows you the layout as it would appear on the device's screen, to help you with design. The *Text view* shows the file as XML text which you can edit. You can go back and forth between the two views and see how your design changes affect XML code, and view versa.

The Palette on your left side (Item #2 in Figure 4.10) contains the different views you can add to the activity. You can drag and drop any item and put it in the middle view to add it. We will not use this technique right now.

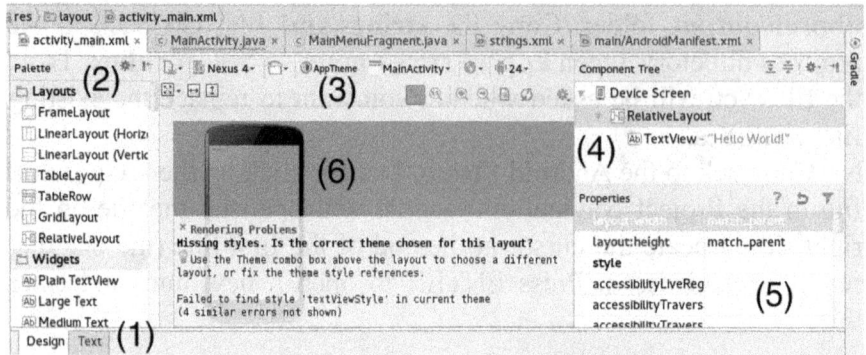

Figure 4.10: Layout View.

The central view (Item #6 in Figure 4.10) shows a problem: the default AppTheme is not suitable for the view. We will change this in a moment.

The Component Tree (Item #4 in Figure 4.10) shows the different views that are on the layout. It also tells you the relationship between the different components, who contains whom, and so on.

When you select a component in the central view or in the Component Tree, the Properties window (Item #5 in Figure 4.10) shows the properties of that component. We will use this later.

Click on the AppTheme button (Item #3 in Figure 4.10) to open the Select Theme dialog box (Figure 4.11). Click on the **DeviceDefault.Light** theme to select it, and click **OK**. Now the error is gone, and the central view shows us the text "Hello World!".

The **Component Tree** on the right shows you that under the main device screen, there is a single **RelativeLayout**. Layouts are the base of any activity's UI, and act as containers for other components of the UI. There are different types of layouts that you can see on the Palette on the left. A **RelativeLayout** is a layout that gives its children relative weight. For example, if you have two views, one to the left and one to the right, and you need the left one to occupy one third of the screen, while the right one occupies the rest, then this layout is your option.

For now, we have only one child, so we don't mind which type of layout we are using. In the future, you will need to consider which type of layout you are using.

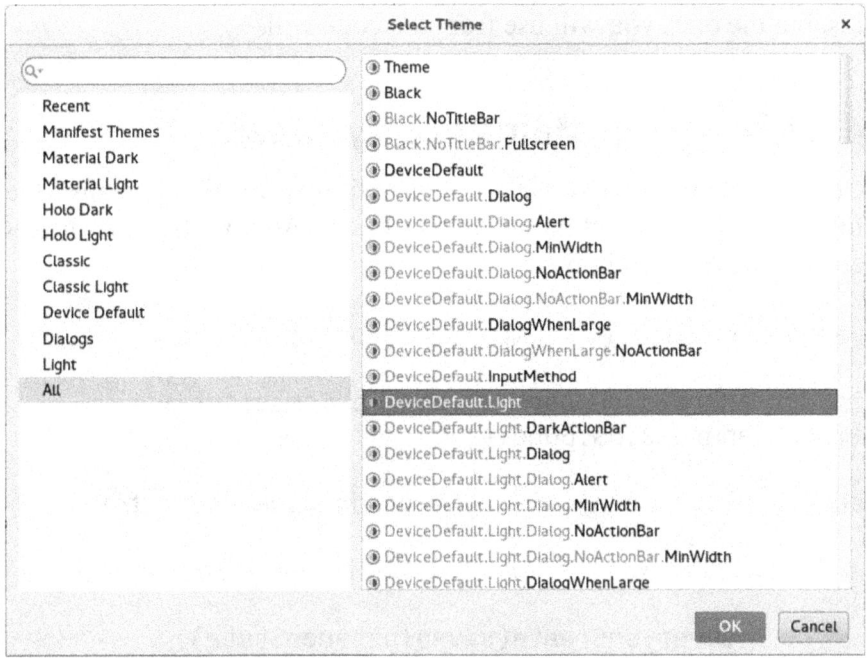

Figure 4.11: The **Select Theme** Dialog Box.

Under the **RelativeLayout** you will find a single child, a **TextView**, which is the view you use when you want to show text to the user. The **TextView** now is showing "Hello World!", this is the magic that made this message appear on the AVD screen when you ran the project earlier.

We don't need this **TextView**, so click on it in the Component Tree or in the central view, and hit Delete on your keyboard. Now the **RelativeLayout** is empty with no children.

Now click on the **RelativeLayout** in the Component Tree, go to the Properties window and scroll down until you find a property named **id**. Click the empty space on the right, and enter: **main_menu_container**, then press ENTER. You will see the word **RelativeLayout** has changed to **main_menu_container** in the Component Tree.

79

The **id** is a unique name you can give to a view component so that you can access it within your Java code. Not all components need ids, but the ones you will use from the code will.

4.5 Fixing the MainActivity Class

Currently, our newly-created MainActivity.java file contains the following lines, added automatically by the Android Studio when it created the main activity:

```
package com.example.www.sampleapplication;

import android.support.v7.app.AppCompatActivity;
import android.os.Bundle;

public class MainActivity extends AppCompatActivity {
    @Override
    protected void onCreate(Bundle savedInstanceState)
{
        super.onCreate(savedInstanceState);
        setContentView(R.layout.activity_main);
    }
}
```

You need to modify the class to look like Listing 4.2. You will need to add lines 12-17 to the existing MainActivity.java class file.

Listing 4.2: MainActivity.java Class Code

```
1     package com.example.www.sampleapplication;
2
3     import android.support.v7.app.AppCompatActivity;
4     import android.os.Bundle;
5
6     public class MainActivity extends
      AppCompatActivity {
7
8         @Override
9         protected void onCreate(Bundle
      savedInstanceState) {
10            super.onCreate(savedInstanceState);
```

```
11          setContentView(R.layout.activity_main);
12
13          MainMenuFragment menu = new
     MainMenuFragment();
14          menu.whoAmI =
     MainMenuFragment.MAIN_MENU;
15          android.app.FragmentTransaction
     transaction =
     getFragmentManager().beginTransaction();

16   transaction.replace(R.id.main_menu_container,
     menu);
17          transaction.commit();
18      }
19  }
```

And here is what the code in Listing 4.2 does:

- Line 9: the onCreate() function is the callback function the Android system calls when it creates your activity the first time.
- Line 10: we call our parent's onCreate() function to let it do whatever start-up it needs. Always do this in your activities.
- Line 11: we tell the system what the layout of our activity should look like. We give it the name of the layout, **R.layout.activity_main** (the same name as the XML file under **res/layouts**) but without the XML extension. The **R** stands for **Resource Class**, a class added dynamically by the Android SDK to your project to let you access your resources.
- Line 13: we create a new instance of the MainMenuFragment class we created in section 4.3.
- line 14: we set the **whoAmI** field of the new MainMenuFragment we created to tell it that we want a main menu, i.e. to view the TOC of the whole book, which is saved under our **strings.xml** file as a string-array called **toc_main**.
- Line 15: to add a fragment to an activity, we need to request a **fragment transaction** from a **fragment manager**. Adding,

updating and removing fragments of activities are all examples of fragment transactions.

- Line 16: we replace the **RelativeLayout** we named **main_menu_container** (see Section 4.4) with the new MainMenuFragment instance we just created.
- Line 17: we commit the changes to make them take effect.

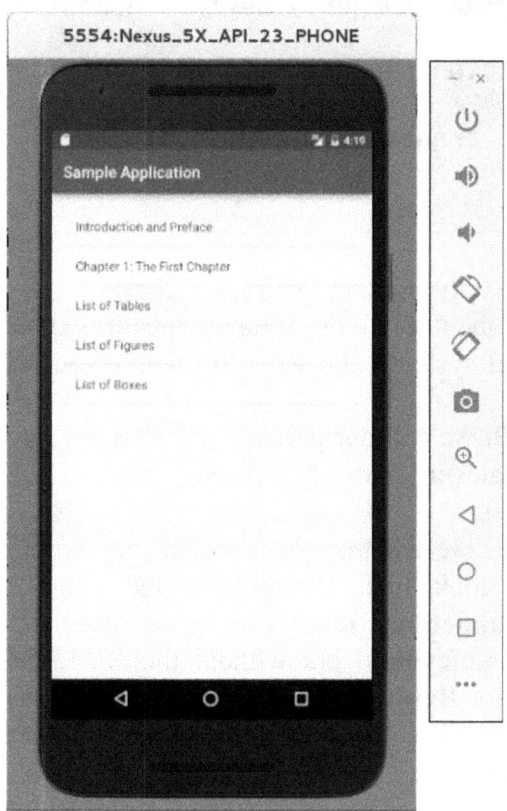

Figure 4.12: SampleApplication Running.

4.6 Testing the SampleApplication on AVD

With the last changes in place, you can test-run the App in your AVD. Click the **Run 'app'** button from the toolbar, or select from the menu **Run → Run 'app'**, or press SHIFT+F10.

It will take a moment for the AVD to boot, but when you go back to the AVD window, it should show you the main Table of Contents (Figure 4.12).

This looks awesome, right?. Unfortunately, it doesn't work yet. Click on any item in the list, and it will do nothing. Let's fix this now.
Open MainMenuFragment.java and go to the line before the the last (If you followed Listing 4.1, go to line 55). This line is the closing line of the loadList() function. Place the cursor at the end of the line, i.e. to the right of the closing brace, and press ENTER to open a new line. Enter the function shown in Listing 4.3. If the Studio asks you if you want to import any classes, click Yes.

Listing 4.3: MainMenuFragment's onListItemClick() function

```
1   @Override
2   public void onListItemClick(ListView l, View v,
    int position, long id) {
3       super.onListItemClick(l, v, position, id);
4       if(this.whoAmI == MAIN_MENU) {
5           String itemName =
    listAdapter.getItem(position);
6           if(itemName.equalsIgnoreCase("list of
    tables")) {
7               MainMenuFragment menu = new
    MainMenuFragment();
8               menu.whoAmI =
    MainMenuFragment.LIST_SUB_MENU;
9               menu.menuIndex = LIST_OF_TABLES;
10              android.app.FragmentTransaction
    transaction =
    getFragmentManager().beginTransaction();
11
    transaction.replace(R.id.main_menu_container,
    menu);
12              transaction.addToBackStack(null);
13              transaction.commit();
14              return;
15          } else if(itemName.equalsIgnoreCase("list
    of figures")) {
16              MainMenuFragment menu = new
    MainMenuFragment();
```

```
17              menu.whoAmI =
     MainMenuFragment.LIST_SUB_MENU;
18              menu.menuIndex = LIST_OF_FIGURES;
19              android.app.FragmentTransaction
     transaction =
     getFragmentManager().beginTransaction();
20
     transaction.replace(R.id.main_menu_container,
     menu);
21              transaction.addToBackStack(null);
22              transaction.commit();
23              return;
24          } else if(itemName.equalsIgnoreCase("list
     of boxes")) {
25              MainMenuFragment menu = new
     MainMenuFragment();
26              menu.whoAmI =
     MainMenuFragment.LIST_SUB_MENU;
27              menu.menuIndex = LIST_OF_BOXES;
28              android.app.FragmentTransaction
     transaction =
     getFragmentManager().beginTransaction();
29
     transaction.replace(R.id.main_menu_container,
     menu);
30              transaction.addToBackStack(null);
31              transaction.commit();
32              return;
33          }
34
35          MainMenuFragment menu = new
     MainMenuFragment();
36          menu.whoAmI = MainMenuFragment.SUB_MENU;
37          menu.menuIndex = position;
38          android.app.FragmentTransaction
     transaction =
     getFragmentManager().beginTransaction();
39
     transaction.replace(R.id.main_menu_container,
     menu);
40          transaction.addToBackStack(null);
41          transaction.commit();
```

```
42      } else if(this.whoAmI == LIST_SUB_MENU) {
43          /* To be done later */
44      } else {
45          /* To be done later */
46      }
47  }
```

And here is what the code in Listing 4.3 does:
- Line 2: this is the function Android calls when a list item is clicked by the user.
- Line 3: call the parent. Always a wise move.
- Line 4: check to see if we are displaying the main menu (the main TOC).
- Line 5: if so, get the actual text of this item.
- Line 6: is this item the "List of Tables"?.
- Lines 7-9: if so, create a new MainMenuFragment instance, tell it that it will view a list, and that list is that of tables.
- Lines 10-11: request a new transaction, then replace the currently viewing fragment with the new one (containing the list of tables).
- Lines 12-14: add the current fragment to the Back Stack, so that when the user presses the Back button from the next fragment, he will be able to come back to the current one. This greatly improves the user experience and your users will greatly appreciate this feature in your App. Then commit the changes and return.
- Lines 15-23: do the same if the clicked item is the List of Figures.
- Lines 24-32: do the same if the clicked item is the List of Boxes.
- Lines 35-41: if all the above failed, that means the user clicked the name of a chapter. We will need to display that chapter's table of contents in the next menu fragment.
- Line 42: check to see if we are currently displaying one of the three lists (of tables, figures or boxes). If so, we need to handle this differently from the above. We will do it later.

- Line 44: if all the above failed, it means the user selected a section from one of the chapters. We will need to retrieve the text of the section from our database and view it to the user. We will do it later also.

Now press CTRL+S (or select **File** → **Save All**) to save your changes. Run the app and try it out. Click on any item in the list and watch the menu change to reflect that. Even the List of Tables, Figures, and Boxes work as expected. Only the sections and the tables, figures and boxes themselves don't show, a behavior we will change soon.

Chapter 5: Adding the Reading Activity

5.1 Adding the DBHelper Class

In order to view our data from the database, we need some way to retrieve data from there. The Android platform provides a helpful SQLite API that helps us with this task. There is a class called **SQLiteOpenHelper** that is there to help us access our database. We will create a class that extends this class.

In the Project Navigation pane on the left side of Android Studio window, double click on **java** to open it. Click on the first item (in our example it reads: **com.example.www.sampleapplication**, select yours if it is different). Right click on it and select **New → Java Class**. In the **Create New Class** dialog box, enter the following:

- Name: **DBHelper**
- Kind: **Class**

The new class is added to the list on the left, and the class file is opened on the right side. Right now, this is an empty class that looks like:

```
package com.example.www.sampleapplication;
/**
 * Created by MIMA on 7/10/16.
 */
public class DBHelper {
}
```

We will fix this now. Make changes to the class file to make it look similar to Listing 5.1. If you copy and paste the code, Android Studio will ask you if you want to import some classes. Select Yes. Basically, you need to modify Line 19, then add Lines 20-91.

Listing 5.1: DBHelper.java Class Code

1	package com.example.www.sampleapplication;
2	
3	import android.content.Context;

```java
import android.database.SQLException;
import android.database.sqlite.SQLiteDatabase;
import android.database.sqlite.SQLiteOpenHelper;
import android.os.Build;
import android.util.Log;

import java.io.File;
import java.io.FileOutputStream;
import java.io.IOException;
import java.io.InputStream;
import java.io.OutputStream;

/**
 * Created by MIMA on 7/10/16.
 */
public class DBHelper extends SQLiteOpenHelper {
    private static String DBPath = "";
    private static String DBName =
"SampleApplicationDB.sqlite";
    private SQLiteDatabase myDB;
    private final Context myContext;
    private static final int DBVersion = 1;
    private final String TAG = "DBHelper";

    public DBHelper(Context context) {
        super(context, DBName, null, DBVersion);
        if(Build.VERSION.SDK_INT >= 17) {
            DBPath =
context.getApplicationInfo().dataDir +
"/databases/";
        } else {
            DBPath = "/data/data/" +
context.getPackageName() + "/databases/";
        }
        this.myContext = context;
    }

    public void createDB() throws IOException {
        boolean DBExists = checkDB();
        if(!DBExists) {
            this.getReadableDatabase();
            this.close();
```

```
42              try {
43                  copyDB();
44                  Log.d(TAG, "Copying database from
   assets");
45              } catch(IOException e) {
46                  throw new Error("Error copying
   DataBase");
47              }
48          }
49      }
50
51      private boolean checkDB() {
52          File file = new File(DBPath + DBName);
53          return file.exists();
54      }
55
56      private void copyDB() throws IOException {
57          InputStream input =
   myContext.getAssets().open(DBName);
58          String outfile = DBPath + DBName;
59          OutputStream output = new
   FileOutputStream(outfile);
60          byte[] buf = new byte[1024];
61          int len;
62          while((len = input.read(buf)) > 0) {
63              output.write(buf, 0, len);
64          }
65          output.flush();
66          output.close();
67          input.close();
68      }
69
70      public boolean openDB() throws SQLException {
71          String path = DBPath + DBName;
72          myDB = SQLiteDatabase.openDatabase(path,
   null, SQLiteDatabase.CREATE_IF_NECESSARY);
73          Log.d(TAG, "Database opened");
74          return myDB != null;
75      }
76
77      @Override
78      public synchronized void close() {
```

```
79          if(myDB != null) myDB.close();
80          super.close();
81      }
82
83      @Override
84      public void onCreate(SQLiteDatabase
    sqLiteDatabase) {
85
86      }
87
88      @Override
89      public void onUpgrade(SQLiteDatabase
    sqLiteDatabase, int i, int i1) {
90
91      }
92 }
```

And here is what the code in Listing 5.1 does:

- Line 19: declare our DBHelper class to be a descendant of SQLiteOpenHelper.
- Line 20: the path to the database file in the internal storage of the target device.
- Line 21: the name of our database file. If you named it differently, change this accordingly.
- Line 22: declare a variable to hold the database we are going to use.
- Line 23: the context of the calling activity.
- Line 24: the version of our database. Start at 1, and increment this every time your make a new version of your app. We should not need to change the version for our eBook app, unless you plan of updating the App, or reusing the App for future versions of your book.
- Line 25: tag required by the debugger for logging debug messages.
- Line 27: the constructor. This function is called whenever a new instance of this class is made.
- Line 28: call the constructor of the parent class (SQLiteOpenHelper), which we pass the context, the name of the required database and its version.

- Lines 29-33: we need to get the path of our application's area in the internal storage of the device. This is different according to the version of the SDK, so we test for this and set the database path accordingly.
- Line 34: we save the context we were passed from our caller.
- Line 37: this function is called when we are to create the database for the first time. *Create* is actually a strong word, what we will actually do is that we will copy the SQLite database we made earlier and copied to the **assets** folder, and copy it into the internal storage of the device, so that our SQLiteOpenHelper can work on it.
- Line 38: we call the `checkDB()` function (line 51) to check if the database is already copied to the internal storage.
- Lines 39-41: if the database doesn't exist, request SQLite to provide us with a readable database.
- Line 43: call `copyDB()` function (line 56) to copy the database file from the **assets** folder to the internal storage.
- Line 44: post a debug message to the log.
- Line 46: if we failed to copy the database, throw an exception (the app will crash and the user will be shown "Application … stopped working").
- Lines 51-54: this function checks if the database file is available in the internal storage and returns a Boolean result accordingly.
- Lines 56-68: this function opens our database file from the **assets** folder for input, opens the database file we created in the internal storage when we requested a readable database on line 40 for output, then copies the input file to output, 1kB at a time (size of the buffer on line 60). It then flushes the output to make sure all data is written to storage, and closes both streams.
- Lines 70-75: this function tries to open the database file in our App's area of the internal storage. It returns a Boolean telling whether the database was successfully opened, and saves a link to the database in the variable we declared on Line 22.
- Lines 78-81: closes the database.

- Line 84: this function is called when the database is created for the first time. We don't need this as our database is pre-made. We just need to make a copy of it.
- Line 89: this function is called when the database is being updated. If you made a newer version of your App, you would need to implement this method to make it update the internal storage's database to reflect the new changes, while preserving the essential data like user's bookmarks and search history, for example.

5.2 Adding the DBAdapter Class

Now we have our DBHelper class in place. In order to link it to the Reading Activity we are about to make, we need an adapter class, which we will call DBAdapter.

In the Project Navigation pane on the left side of Android Studio window, double click on **java** to open it. Click on the first item (in our example it reads: **com.example.www.sampleapplication**, select yours if it is different). Right click on it and select **New → Java Class**. In the **Create New Class** dialog box, enter the following:

- Name: **DBAdapter**
- Kind: **Class**

The new class is added to the list on the left, and the class file is opened on the right side. Right now, this is an empty class that looks like:

```
package com.example.www.sampleapplication;
/**
 * Created by MIMA on 7/10/16.
 */
public class DBAdapter {
}
```

We will fix this now. Make changes to the class file to make it look similar to Listing 5.2. If you copy and paste the code, Android Studio will ask you if you want to import some classes. Select Yes. Basically, you need to add Lines 15-90.

Listing 5.2: DBAdapter.java Class Code

```
1    package com.example.www.sampleapplication;
2
3    import android.content.Context;
4    import android.database.Cursor;
5    import android.database.SQLException;
6    import android.database.sqlite.SQLiteDatabase;
7    import android.util.Log;
8
9    import java.io.IOException;
10
11   /**
12    * Created by MIMA on 7/10/16.
13    */
14   public class DBAdapter {
15       private final Context myContext;
16       private SQLiteDatabase myDB;
17       private DBHelper myDBHelper;
18       private final String TAG = "DBAdapter";
19
20       public DBAdapter(Context context) {
21           this.myContext = context;
22           myDBHelper = new DBHelper(myContext);
23       }
24
25       public DBAdapter createDB() throws
     SQLException {
26           try {
27               myDBHelper.createDB();
28           } catch(IOException e) {
29               throw new Error("Failed to create
     DataBase");
30           }
31           return this;
32       }
33
34       public DBAdapter open() throws SQLException {
35           try {
36               myDBHelper.openDB();
37               myDBHelper.close();
38               myDB =
     myDBHelper.getReadableDatabase();
```

```java
39              } catch(SQLException e) {
40                  throw e;
41              }
42              return this;
43          }
44
45      public void close() {
46          myDBHelper.close();
47      }
48
49      public Cursor getData(String boxOrFootnote,
    char type) {
50              String query;
51              if(type == LoadingTask.REQUEST_FOOTNOTE)
    {
52                  query = "SELECT * FROM 'Footnotes'
    WHERE Title = '" + boxOrFootnote + "';";
53              } else if(type ==
    LoadingTask.REQUEST_BOX) {
54                  query = "SELECT * FROM 'Boxes' WHERE
    Title = '" + boxOrFootnote + "';";
55              } else return null;
56              Log.d(TAG, "query: " + query);
57
58              try {
59                  Cursor cur = myDB.rawQuery(query,
    null);
60                  return cur;
61              } catch (SQLException e) {
62                  throw e;
63              }
64          }
65
66      public Cursor getData(String tableName) {
67          try {
68              String query = "SELECT * FROM '" +
    tableName + "';";
69              Log.d(TAG, "query: " + query);
70
71              Cursor cur = myDB.rawQuery(query,
    null);
72              return cur;
```

94

```
73              } catch (SQLException e) {
74                  throw e;
75              }
76          }
77
78      public Cursor getData(int chap, int section)
        {
79          try {
80              String tableName =
        myContext.getResources().getString(R.string.book_
        table_name);
81              String query = "SELECT * FROM " +
        tableName + " WHERE " +
82                      "Chapter = " + chap + " AND
        SectionHead = " + section + ";";
83              Log.d(TAG, "query: " + query);
84
85              Cursor cur = myDB.rawQuery(query,
        null);
86              return cur;
87          } catch (SQLException e) {
88              throw e;
89          }
90      }
91  }
```

And here is what the code in Listing 5.2 does:

- Line 15: the context that is passed to us from our caller. We will pass it to the DBHelper class who will handle the database.
- Line 16: the database we will be using.
- Line 17: the DBHelper class instance we will call to access the database.
- Line 18: tag required by the debugger for logging debug messages.
- Line 20: the constructor method which is called whenever a new instance of this class is created.
- Line 21: save the instance of the context that is passed to us.
- Line 22: create a new instance of the DBHelper class.

- Lines 25-32: this function creates the database if it is the first time the application is run. It actually calls the `createDB()` function of the DBHelper class who will do all the dirty work.
- Lines 34-43: this function opens the database for reading.
- Lines 45-47: this function closes the open database by calling DBHelper class's `close()` function.
- Lines 49-90: these three are overloaded versions of the same function, `getData()`, which is the main function we will use later to fetch data from the database. In the first version, we fetch data from either the Footnotes or the Boxes tables in the database. In the second version, we fetch a complete Table, like table0, table1 and so on. In the third version, we fetch a section, given the chapter and section numbers. We need three different functions because the SQL query string will differ according to the requested data.

If you look at lines 51 and 53 in your Android Studio, you will see that the word **LoadingTask** is displayed in red, because the Studio couldn't figure it out. If you hover the mouse over it, it will show: *Cannot Resolve Symbol 'LoadingTask'*. If you position the cursor over it and press ALT+ENTER, the Studio will give you some suggestions to remedy it. Select the first item, *Create Class 'LoadingTask'* and press Enter. A dialog box shows (Figure 5.1). Don't change anything and click **OK**. The new, empty, class file is opened, and it reads:

```
package com.example.www.sampleapplication;

/**
 * Created by MIMA on 7/10/16.
 */
public class LoadingTask {
}
```

We are going to fix this class in the next section.

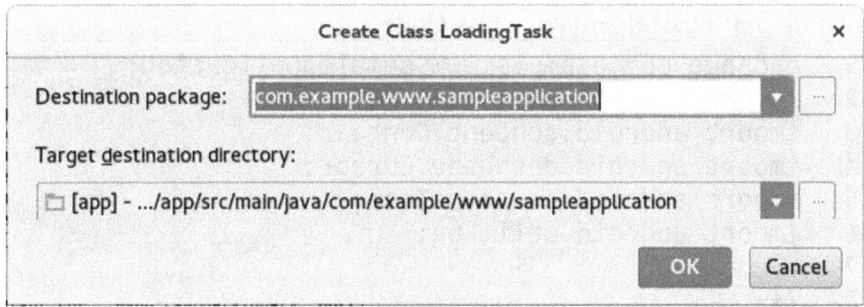

Figure 5.1: The **Create Class** Dialog Box.

5.3 Editing the LoadingTask Class

Loading data from a database is usually a heavy task that consumes time and CPU cycles. That means if you access a database from the foreground thread of execution (the thing that the user sees on the screen), it is probable that the user interface will freeze, or at best slow down. The user is never happy with a freezing UI, especially if he doesn't know why it happened. He will probably think that your App is buggy and maybe he will remove it.

For these reasons it is advisable to do database-related functions in a background thread, and leave the foreground thread to handle UI. You will probably need to provide the user with a progress dialog to show the progress of the background task, be it downloading a file from the internet, reading data from a database, or whatever the background task is doing.

We are going to handle our database access using a class named AsyncTask, which stands for Asynchronous Task. The task runs in the background, and when it finishes it calls the activity that started the task to let it now it finished its work.

You need to make changes to the LoadingTask class to make it similar to Listing 5.3. If you copy and paste the code, Android Studio will ask you if you want to import some classes. Select Yes. Basically, you need to modify Line 11, then add Lines 12-66.

Listing 5.3: DBHelper.java Class Code

```
1   package com.example.www.sampleapplication;
2
3   import android.content.Context;
4   import android.database.Cursor;
5   import android.os.AsyncTask;
6   import android.util.Log;
7
8   /**
9    * Created by MIMA on 7/10/16.
10   */
11  public class LoadingTask extends AsyncTask {
12      int chap, section;
13      String table;
14      String boxOrFootnote;
15      Context myContext;
16      private ReadingActivity parentRA;
17      private final String TAG = "LoadingTask";
18      private char request;
19      public static final char REQUEST_CHAP_SECTION
    = 1;
20      public static final char REQUEST_TABLE = 2;
21      public static final char REQUEST_FOOTNOTE =
    3;
22      public static final char REQUEST_BOX = 4;
23      public static final char REQUEST_FIGURE = 5;
24
25      public interface LoadingTaskFinishedListener
    {
26          void onTaskFinished(Cursor cursor);
27      }
28
29      private final LoadingTaskFinishedListener
    finishedListener;
30
31      public
    LoadingTask(LoadingTaskFinishedListener
    finishedListener, ReadingActivity parent,
32                          int chap, int section) {
33          this.finishedListener = finishedListener;
34          this.chap = chap;
35          this.section = section;
```

```
36         this.myContext = parent.getBaseContext();
37         this.parentRA = parent;
38         this.request = REQUEST_CHAP_SECTION;
39     }
40
41     @Override
42     protected void onPreExecute() {
43         super.onPreExecute();
44     }
45
46     @Override
47     protected Object doInBackground(Object[]
    objects) {
48         DBAdapter dbadapter = new
    DBAdapter(myContext);
49         dbadapter.createDB();
50         dbadapter.open();
51         Cursor cur = null;
52         if(this.request == REQUEST_CHAP_SECTION)
53             cur = dbadapter.getData(chap,
    section);
54         else if(this.request == REQUEST_TABLE)
55             cur = dbadapter.getData(table);
56         else
57             cur =
    dbadapter.getData(this.boxOrFootnote,
    this.request);
58         Log.d(TAG, "got " + cur.getCount() + "
    rows");
59         return cur;
60     }
61
62     @Override
63     protected void onPostExecute(Object o) {
64         super.onPostExecute(o);
65         finishedListener.onTaskFinished((Cursor)
    o);
66     }
67 }
```

And here is what the code in Listing 5.3 does:
- Line 11: declare this class to be descendant from AsyncTask,

99

the class that handles background asynchronous tasks.

- Line 12: if we are called to load a section from the book, we save chapter and section numbers in those variables.
- Line 13: if we are called to load a table, this variable holds the name of the table, e.g. table0, table1, ...
- Line 14: if we are called to load a side-box or a footnote, this variable holds the name of the box or footnote, e.g. fnote1, box3, ...
- Line 15: the context we will pass to DBAdapter.
- Line 16: the parent who called us. Right now, the ReadingActivity class is not implemented, so this will be shown in red. We will fix it later.
- Line 17: tag required by the debugger for logging debug messages.
- Line 18: what the caller wants us to load? A table? A section from a chapter? Anything else? The possible values for the **request** variable are defined in the lines 19-23.
- Lines 19-23: the possible values for the **request** variable.
- Line 25: this interface defines how this class can communicate with caller classes. Any class who wants to call use must implement this interface with its function(s).
- Line 26: any class who wants to use our service must implement this function. We will call it when we finish the loading task.
- Line 29: here we will save the instance of the class who called us so that we can call it's `onTaskFinished()` function when we finish.
- Lines 31-39: this is the constructor method which is called whenever a new instance of this class is created. It must be passed the class whom we will call after we finish, the parent who called us (usually the same as the first argument), the requested chapter and section numbers. We save all of them in our local variables for later access.
- Line 42: function that is called before the background process starts. We don't need to do anything in it, so we just call the parent's function.
- Line 47: the main function that does the donkey work of this

class.

- Line 48: create a new instance of the DBAdapter class, which will handle our database access.
- Lines 49-50: create (if it's the first time) and open the database.
- Line 51: the Cursor object which will hold the result of our SQL query.
- Line 52: we check if we were requested to fetch a section of a chapter. Currently, this is the only option that actually works.
- Line 53: tell our database adapter to fetch the requested section.
- Lines 54-55: check if we were requested to fetch a table and gets it.
- Lines 56-57: otherwise, we were requested to fetch a footnote or a side-box. Get it.
- Line 58: write out a debug message to the log.
- Line 59: return the result of the SQL query in a Cursor object to the caller.
- Lines 63-66: this is the function Android calls when the `doInBackground()` function finishes. We will call our parent's `onPostExecute()` and then call the caller to tell it we finished our work.

If you look at lines 16 and 31 in your Android Studio, you will see that the word **ReadingActivity** is displayed in red, because the Studio couldn't figure it out. If you hover the mouse over it, it will show: *Cannot Resolve Symbol 'ReadingActivity'*. If you position the cursor over it and press ALT+ENTER, the Studio will give you some suggestions to remedy it. Select the first item, *Create Class 'ReadingActivity'* and press Enter. A dialog box shows (similar to that in Figure 5.1). Don't change anything and click **OK**. The new, empty, class file is opened, and it reads:

```
package com.example.www.sampleapplication;

/**
 * Created by MIMA on 7/10/16.
```

```
*/
public class ReadingActivity {
}
```

We are going to fix this, right after we add another layout file.

5.4 Adding activity_reading.xml Layout

In the Project Navigation pane on the left side of Android Studio, double click on **res** to open it. Right click on **layout**, and select **New → Layout Resource File**. The **New Resource File** dialog box opens (Figure 5.2).

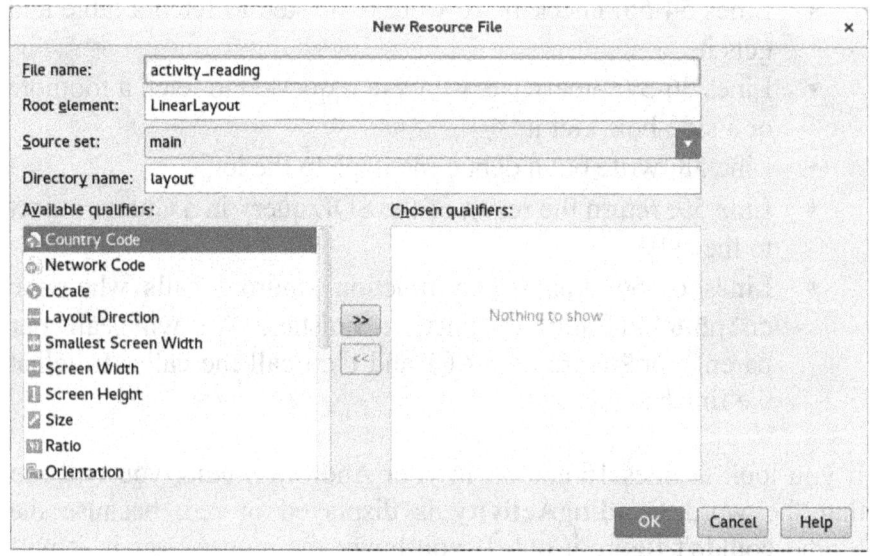

Figure 5.2: The **New Resource File** Dialog Box.

Enter the following in the dialog box:
- File name: **activity_reading**
- Root element: **LinearLayout**
- Source set: **main**
- Directory name: **Layout**

And press **OK**. The new layout opens in the layout view. Change the

theme (by clicking on AppTheme button, Item #3 in Figure 4.10).
Select **DeviceDefault.Light** and click **OK**.

Switch the view to *Text* (Item #1 in Figure 4.10). This will show you
the XML version of the **activity_reading** layout. It reads like:

```
<?xml version="1.0" encoding="utf-8"?>
<LinearLayout
xmlns:android="http://schemas.android.com/apk/res/and
roid"
    android:orientation="vertical"
android:layout_width="match_parent"
    android:layout_height="match_parent">
</LinearLayout>
```

Edit the file to look like Listing 5.4. We would usually edit layouts in
the *Design* mode, but in this particular case, it would be easier and
quicker to edit (or copy and paste) the XML code directly.

Listing 5.4: activity_reading.xml File

```
1   <?xml version="1.0" encoding="utf-8"?>
2   <LinearLayout
    xmlns:android="http://schemas.android.com/apk/res
    /android"
3       android:orientation="vertical"
    android:layout_width="match_parent"
4       android:layout_height="match_parent"
5       android:id="@+id/reading_layout">
6
7       <LinearLayout
8           android:orientation="horizontal"
9           android:layout_width="match_parent"
10          android:layout_height="wrap_content"
11          android:id="@+id/linearLayout"
12
    android:background="@color/button_material_light"
13          android:layout_gravity="top">
14
15          <ImageButton
16              android:layout_width="wrap_content"
17              android:layout_height="wrap_content"
```

```
18              android:id="@+id/font_inc_button"
19              android:clickable="true"
20              android:src="@mipmap/ic_action_plus"
21
    android:onClick="onFontIncButtonClickReadingActiv
    ity"
22              android:layout_gravity="left" />
23
24          <ImageButton
25              android:layout_width="wrap_content"
26              android:layout_height="wrap_content"
27              android:id="@+id/font_dec_button"
28              android:src="@mipmap/ic_action_minus"
29
    android:onClick="onFontDecButtonClickReadingActiv
    ity" />
30
31          <Spinner
32              android:layout_width="0dp"
33              android:layout_height="match_parent"
34
    android:id="@+id/reading_chap_name_list"
35              android:layout_weight="1"
36              android:clickable="true" />
37
38          <ImageButton
39              android:layout_width="wrap_content"
40              android:layout_height="wrap_content"
41              android:id="@+id/prevButton"
42
    android:src="@android:drawable/ic_media_rew"
43
    android:onClick="onPrevButtonClickReadingActivity
    " />
44
45          <TextView
46              android:layout_width="wrap_content"
47              android:layout_height="match_parent"
48              android:text=" 1 "
49
    android:id="@+id/reading_section_number"
50              android:gravity="center" />
```

```
51        <ImageButton
52            android:layout_width="wrap_content"
53            android:layout_height="wrap_content"
54            android:id="@+id/nextButton"
55            android:layout_gravity="right"
56
android:src="@android:drawable/ic_media_ff"
57
android:onClick="onNextButtonClickReadingActivity
58    " />
59
60      </LinearLayout>
61
62      <ScrollView
63          android:layout_width="match_parent"
64          android:layout_height="match_parent"
65          android:id="@+id/scrollView"

66  android:layout_gravity="center_horizontal" >
67
68          <TextView
69              android:layout_width="wrap_content"
70              android:layout_height="wrap_content"
71              android:text=""
72              android:id="@+id/reading_text" />
73      </ScrollView>
74  </LinearLayout>
```

Essentially, what Listing 5.4 is doing is that it creates a vertical **LinearLayout** (with the **id:** reading_layout) with two children: the first is a horizontal **LinearLayout** (with the **id:** linearLayout) that will function as our toolbar, the second is a **ScrollView** (with the **id:** scrollView) that will contain the actual reading area.

The toolbar contains the following components:

- *font_inc_button:* an ImageButton that will show a searching glass icon with a big plus in the middle. When the user clicks this button it should enlarge the font size of the text.
- *font_dec_button:* an ImageButton that will show a searching glass icon with a big minus in the middle. When the user clicks this button it should reduce the font size of the text.

- *reading_chap_name_list:* a Spinner (Android's version of a drop-down list, or a ComboBox if you are Windows-born) that will show the section names of the current chapter. The user can select any section from this list and we should fetch it from the database and show it.
- *prevButton:* an ImageButton that shows backward arrows. When clicked it should take us to the previous section in this chapter. If we are at the first section, it should take us to the last section of the previous chapter.
- *reading_section_number:* a TextView that will display the number of the current section and the total number of sections within the current chapter.
- *nextButton:* an ImageButton that shows forward arrows. When clicked it should take us to the next section in this chapter. If we are at the final section, it should take us to the first section of the next chapter.

The scrollView component contains one child, a TextView with the id: reading_text. This is where we display the section text we fetched from the database.

There is only one problem now: the icons we need for **font_inc_button** and **font_dec_button** are missing. You can provide them, but you will need to provide different icons for the different possible screen sizes. Otherwise, download my two icons from: http://sites.google.com/site/mohammedisam2000/home/action_icons .zip

Unpack the zipped file somewhere in your home directory. Open the unpacked folder, you will find **mipmap** folders that correspond to the **mipmap** folders in your project's directory. Each one of them contains two files: **ic_action_plus.png** and **ic_action_minus.png**. The different files contain the same icons but in different resolutions, to match different screen densities. Copy the files within each folder to its corresponding folder in your application's **app/src/main/res** folder.

5.5 Editing the ReadingActivity Class

We are going to fix the ReadingActivity class you added at the end of section 5.3. Double click the **ReadingActivity** class name under **java** in the Project Navigation pane to open the class file. Edit the file to make it look like Listing 5.5. If you copy and paste the code, Android Studio will ask you if you want to import some classes. Select Yes. Basically, you need to modify Line 21, then add Lines 22-157.

Listing 5.5: ReadingActivity.java Class Code

```
1    package com.example.www.sampleapplication;
2
3    import android.app.ProgressDialog;
4    import android.database.Cursor;
5    import android.os.Bundle;
6    import android.support.annotation.Nullable;
7    import
     android.support.v7.app.AppCompatActivity;
8    import android.text.Html;
9    import android.text.method.LinkMovementMethod;
10   import android.util.DisplayMetrics;
11   import android.util.Log;
12   import android.view.View;
13   import android.widget.AdapterView;
14   import android.widget.ArrayAdapter;
15   import android.widget.Spinner;
16   import android.widget.TextView;
17
18   /**
19    * Created by MIMA on 7/10/16.
20    */
21   public class ReadingActivity extends
     AppCompatActivity implements
     LoadingTask.LoadingTaskFinishedListener {
22       String PackageName;
23       int chap, section, sectionCount;
24       ProgressDialog PD;
25       private TextView sectionNumView;
26       private Spinner chapNameView;
27       private static final String TAG =
```

```
                    "ReadingActivity";
28
29          @Override
30          protected void onCreate(@Nullable Bundle
        savedInstanceState) {
31              super.onCreate(savedInstanceState);
32
        setContentView(R.layout.activity_reading);
33              PackageName =
        getApplicationContext().getPackageName();
34
35              chap =
        getIntent().getIntExtra(PackageName + ".chap",
        0);
36              section =
        getIntent().getIntExtra(PackageName +
        ".section", 0);
37
38              PD = new
        ProgressDialog(ReadingActivity.this);
39              PD.setTitle("Please wait");
40              PD.setMessage("Loading...");
41              PD.setCancelable(false);
42              PD.show();
43              setSubTitle();
44              sectionNumView =
        (TextView)findViewById(R.id.reading_section_num
        ber);
45              chapNameView =
        (Spinner)findViewById(R.id.reading_chap_name_li
        st);
46
47          /* set the event handler for the
        Chapters drop-down list */
48
        chapNameView.setOnItemSelectedListener(new
        AdapterView.OnItemSelectedListener() {
49              @Override
50              public void
        onItemSelected(AdapterView<?> adapterView, View
        view, int i, long l) {
51                  PD.show();
```

```
52              section = i;
53              new
LoadingTask(ReadingActivity.this,
ReadingActivity.this, chap, section).execute();
54           }
55
56           @Override
57           public void
onNothingSelected(AdapterView<?> adapterView) {
58
59           }
60       });
61
62       getSectionNames(this.section);
63   }
64
65   @Override
66   public void onTaskFinished(Cursor cursor) {
67       TextView textView =
(TextView)findViewById(R.id.reading_text);
68
textView.setMovementMethod(LinkMovementMethod.g
etInstance());
69       cursor.moveToFirst();
70       String textbody =
cursor.getString(cursor.getColumnIndexOrThrow("
BodyText"));
71
textView.setText(Html.fromHtml(textbody));
72
sectionNumView.setText(Integer.toString(this.se
ction + 1) + "/" + this.sectionCount);
73       if(PD.isShowing()) PD.dismiss();
74   }
75
76   public void
onFontIncButtonClickReadingActivity(View view)
{
77       TextView txt =
(TextView)findViewById(R.id.reading_text);
78       DisplayMetrics metrics =
getApplicationContext().getResources().getDispl
```

```
79        ayMetrics();
          float sz =
      txt.getTextSize()/metrics.density;
80        if(sz < 40.0F) {
81            txt.setTextSize(sz + 1.0F);
82        }
83    }
84
85    public void
      onFontDecButtonClickReadingActivity(View view)
      {
86        TextView txt =
      (TextView)findViewById(R.id.reading_text);
87        DisplayMetrics metrics =
      getApplicationContext().getResources().getDispl
      ayMetrics();
88        float sz =
      txt.getTextSize()/metrics.density;
89        if(sz > 10.0F) {
90            txt.setTextSize(sz - 1.0F);
91        }
92    }
93
94    public void
      onNextButtonClickReadingActivity(View view) {
95        Log.d(TAG, section + ", " +
      sectionCount);
96        if(section < sectionCount-1) {
97            section++;
98
      chapNameView.setSelection(chapNameView.getSelec
      tedItemPosition() + 1);
99        } else {
100           if(chap < getTOCSize()-1) {
101               chap++;
102               setSubTitle();
103               getSectionNames(0);
104           } else {
105               return;
106           }
107       }
108
```

```
     sectionNumView.setText(Integer.toString(this.se
     ction + 1) + "/" + this.sectionCount);
109      }
110
111      public void
     onPrevButtonClickReadingActivity(View view) {
112          if(section > 0) {
113              section--;
114
     chapNameView.setSelection(chapNameView.getSelec
     tedItemPosition() - 1);
115          } else {
116              if(chap > 0) {
117                  chap--;
118                  setSubTitle();
119                  getSectionCount();
120
     getSectionNames(this.sectionCount-1);
121              } else {
122                  return;
123              }
124          }
125
     sectionNumView.setText(Integer.toString(this.se
     ction + 1) + "/" + this.sectionCount);
126      }
127
128      void setSubTitle() {
129          String toc_name = "toc_main";
130          String[] toc =
     getResources().getStringArray(getResources().ge
     tIdentifier(toc_name,
131                  "array", PackageName));
132
     getSupportActionBar().setSubtitle(toc[this.chap
     ]);
133      }
134
135      int getTOCSize() {
136          String toc_name = "toc_main";
137          String[] toc =
     getResources().getStringArray(getResources().ge
```

```
tIdentifier(toc_name,
138                "array", PackageName));
139         return toc.length;
140     }
141
142     void getSectionCount() {
143         String toc_name = "toc_" +
144  Integer.toString(chap);
          String[] toc =
     getResources().getStringArray(getResources().ge
     tIdentifier(toc_name,
145                "array", PackageName));
146         this.sectionCount = toc.length;
147     }
148
149     void getSectionNames(int setSelection) {
150         String toc_name = "toc_" +
     Integer.toString(chap);
151         String[] toc =
     getResources().getStringArray(getResources().ge
     tIdentifier(toc_name,
152                "array", PackageName));
153         this.sectionCount = toc.length;
154         ArrayAdapter arr = new
     ArrayAdapter(this,
     android.R.layout.simple_spinner_item, toc);
155         chapNameView.setAdapter(arr);
156
     chapNameView.setSelection(setSelection);
157     }
158  }
```

And here is what the code in Listing 5.5 does:

- Line 21: declare this class as a descendant of AppCompatActivity, which means it is an activity. Also this class implements the LoadingTaskFinishedListener interface which we need in order to communicate with the LoadingTask class.
- Line 22: a variable to save the package name string in.
- Line 23: variables to save the chapter number, section number, and the count of sections in the current chapter.

112

- Line 24: a progress dialog we will show to the user while we are loading from the database.
- Line 25: a link to the **reading_section_number** TextView that we added to **activity_reading.xml** earlier.
- Line 26: a link to the **reading_chap_name_list** Spinner that we added to **activity_reading.xml** earlier.
- Line 27: tag required by the debugger for logging debug messages.
- Line 30: this is the function that Android system will call whenever it creates a new instance of this activity.
- Line 31: always call the parent's `onCreate()` function.
- Line 32: tell the system what layout to use as the UI of this activity.
- Line 33: get the package name from the application.
- Lines 35-36: get the intent that was used to start this activity, then retrieve the chapter number and the section number from it. We will need them when we read from the database.
- Lines 38-42: we create a progress dialog, set its title and body message, then show it to the user.
- Line 43: we call the `setSubTitle()` function (defined on line 128) to set the subtitle of this activity, which is shown on the action bar.
- Line 44: get the **reading_section_number** TextView that we added to **activity_reading.xml** earlier.
- Line 45: get the **reading_chap_name_list** Spinner that we added to **activity_reading.xml** earlier.
- Lines 48-60: we add an event handler (also known as an action listener). What it does is that it *listens* to a certain event, in this case when an item in the sections list is selected. When this happens, the action listener shows a progress dialog to the user, then creates a new LoadingTask class, telling it who we are and what chapter and section we need it to load.
- Line 62: update the drop-down section list by calling the function defined on line 149.
- Line 66: this is the function our LoadingTask class will call after it finishes its background activity.

- Line 67: get the TextView on which we will show the acquired text.
- Line 68: this call is important to make the TextView enable clicking on links inside the text. We embed links in the text as HTML hyperlinks. When the user clicks a link, it will open a table, a figure, a footnote, a side-box, or even an external website link.
- Line 69: we will move to the first row in the Cursor that holds our data to make sure we view the right data.
- Line 70: we select the **BodyText** field from the data, we don't need the rest of fields (namely: Chapter, SectionHead, and _id, remember Chapter 3?).
- Line 71: set the TextView's text to the result we obtained from the database, but first make sure it is formatted as HTML so that the links are viewed as real, clickable links.
- Line 72: set the text of the **reading_section_number** TextView to show the number of this section, and the total number of sections in this chapter.
- Line 73: don't forget to dismiss the progress dialog if it is still showing.
- Line 76: this function is called when the **font_inc_button** is clicked (we made this link on Line 21 of Listing 5.4).
- Line 77: get the **reading_text** TextView.
- Lines 78-82: we want to increase the font size by 1. But the getTextSize() function returns the real pixel dimensions of the text, while the setTextSize() function accepts sizes in scaled pixels, which would be different for each screen density (ldpi, mdpi, ...). This is why we need to scale the current font size by the current screen density before adding 1 and passing the value to setTextSize().
- line 85: this function is called when the **font_dec_button** is clicked (we made this link on Line 29 of Listing 5.4).
- Lines 86-91: does the same as the font increment function above, only it decreases the font size.
- Lines 94-109: this is the function that is called when the **nextButton** is clicked (we made this link on Line 58 of Listing 5.4). The function first checks if there are more

114

sections in the chapter. If there is, it goes to the next section and updates the **chapNameView** spinner to show the new section name as the selection. If there are no more sections in the chapter, it checks if there is another chapter after this one. If there is, it goes to the next chapter, sets section number to zero, and updates the the **chapNameView** spinner. The action listener we defined on lines 48-60 will do the work of fetching the new section from the database and updating the **reading_text** TextView.

- Lines 111-126: this is the function that is called when **prevButton** is clicked (we made this link on Line 43 of Listing 5.4). The function first checks if we hit the first section in the chapter or not. If not, it goes to the previous section and updates the **chapNameView** spinner to show the new section name as the selection. If this is the first section in the chapter, it checks if this is the first chapter. If it is not, it goes to the previous chapter, sets the section number to the last section in the previous chapter, and updates the the **chapNameView** spinner. The action listener we defined on lines 48-60 will do the work of fetching the new section from the database and updating the **reading_text** TextView.

- Lines 128-133: this function sets the subtitle of this activity. It gets the main TOC from string resources, which **dbprep** has saved for us in a string-array named **toc_main**. The function gets this array and fetches from it the name of the current chapter and displays it as the subtitle.

- Lines 135-140: this function gets the size of **toc_main** string array, which essentially tells us how many items are there in the TOC.

- Lines 142-147: this function gets the number of sections in the current chapter. It gets the string-array corresponding to the current chapter. It then gets the length of this array, which is the number of sections in the specified chapter.

- Lines 149-157: this function gets the section names of the current chapter, loads them into the **chapNameView** spinner, then sets the spinner's selected item as requested. Remember that the action listener of the spinner will do the work of loading the section into view.

5.6 Editing the MainMenuFragment Class

Our reading activity is ready, but we need to connect it to our main menu, so that when the user clicks on a chapter's section, this action leads to opening the reading activity and displaying the said section. In the Project Navigation pane, double click on **MainMenuFragment** to open it on the right side. Scroll down to line 105 where we had previously put:

```
/* To be done later */
```

Delete this line, and insert instead:

```
Intent myIntent = new Intent();
myIntent.setClass(getActivity(),
ReadingActivity.class);
myIntent.putExtra(PackageName + ".chap", menuIndex);
myIntent.putExtra(PackageName + ".section",
position);
startActivity(myIntent);
```

What the code does is that:
- It gets a new Intent object.
- It sets the class of the intent to be of the ReadingActivity class. Remember from Chapter 2 that this makes it an explicit intent.
- It then adds the chapter and section numbers, which the ReadingActivity class will need to fetch the required data from our database.
- It then fires the intent to start the ReadingActivity and display the section the user selected.

5.7 Editing AndroidManifest.xml

If you go on and try the app right now, and click on a section in the TOC, the app will crash with an **ActivityNotFoundException** (shown in the LogCat debugger at the bottom, in red, as shown in

Figure 5.3). This happened because you didn't declare the reading activity in your manifest file. And remember: any undeclared activity is a non-existent activity, as far as the Android system is concerned.

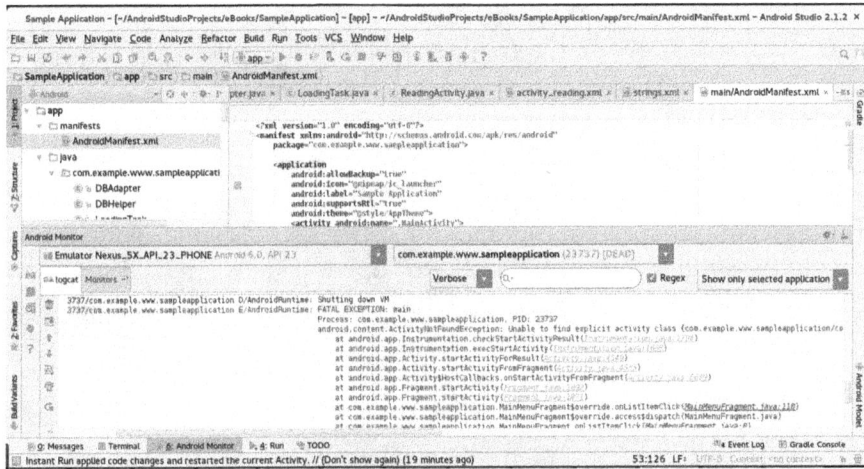

Figure 5.3: The LogCat Debugger Showing Crash Report.

In order to avoid this, you need to declare the activity in your manifest file. Double click **manifests** in the Project Navigation pane to open the manifest file, which should read:

```
1   <?xml version="1.0" encoding="utf-8"?>
2   <manifest
    xmlns:android="http://schemas.android.com/apk/re
    s/android"
3       package="com.example.www.sampleapplication">
4
5       <application
6           android:allowBackup="true"
7           android:icon="@mipmap/ic_launcher"
8           android:label="@string/app_name"
9           android:supportsRtl="true"
10          android:theme="@style/AppTheme">
11          <activity android:name=".MainActivity">
12              <intent-filter>
13                  <action
    android:name="android.intent.action.MAIN" />
```

```
14
15                        <category
      android:name="android.intent.category.LAUNCHER"
      />
16                     </intent-filter>
17               </activity>
18          </application>
19
20    </manifest>
```

Position the cursor at the end of line 17 (the one that reads:
</activity>) and press ENTER to open a new line. Enter the
following between this line and the current line 18 (the one that
reads: </application>):

```
<activity android:name=".ReadingActivity"
    android:parentActivityName=".MainActivity">
    <!-- to support navigation on Android older than
4.1 (API level 16) -->
    <meta-data
        android:name="android.support.PARENT_ACTIVITY"
        android:value=".MainActivity"></meta-data>
</activity>
```

This declares the ReadingActivity to the Android system so that it
can be called and run. It also tells whose the parent activity of it is,
so that a Back to parent arrow can be displayed on the Action bar to
return the user to the main menu.

Notice that this activity declaration is not like the MainActivity one
(lines 11-17 in the above Listing). The main activity of your App
should declare a special intent-filter. Intent filters tell the Android
system what type of intents the activity is able to receive. If, for
example, you have an activity that can play videos, you should
declare that your activity can play videos by including an intent-filter
that shows that.

The main activity must have an intent-filter that tells it receives the
action   ACTION_MAIN,   of   the   category
CATEGORY_LAUNCHER. If it doesn't declare *both* of those two
fields explicitly, your App would not be shown on the application
launcher menu, and the user could not start it.

Now your app is ready to run. Run it and try it on the AVD. Click on Chapter 1 and select one of the sections. It should fire a ReadingActivity and show the selected section. Click the Back button and try another section. Try the font plus and minus buttons. Try to change sections by using the spinner and the buttons. Pretty nice, right?.

Still though, we didn't implement the activity that will react to the links, so if you click on any table, figure, box or footnote link it won't do anything. We are going to fix this in the next chapter.

Chapter 6: Adding the TableView Class

6.1 A Word on URIs

The word URI stands for Universal Resource Identifier, which is a protocol for finding things (mainly data from our point of view). It is closely related to URL, the Universal Resource Locator, the URL being a sub-category of the URI. Hence, every URL is a URI, but not every URI is a URL.

You can read more on http://www.ietf.org/rfc/rfc2396.txt.

We will not get into details of URIs, but in general, a URI takes the form:

```
[scheme:][//authority][path][?query][#fragment]
```

There is a class named *Uri* in the Android API library that can be used to manipulate URIs. We are going to use this when we will need to call the TableActivity that we will define in the next section.

6.2 Adding the TableView Class

In the Project Navigation pane on the left, double click **java**, then right click on the first item (in our sample project it reads: *com.example.www.sampleapplication*) and select **New → Java Class**. In the **Create New Class** dialog box, enter the following:
- Name: **TableView**
- Kind: **Class**

The new class is added to the list on the left, and the class file is opened on the right side. Right now, this is an empty class that looks like:

```
package com.example.www.sampleapplication;

/**
```

```
* Created by MIMA on 7/10/16.
*/
public class TableView {
}
```

Edit the file to make it look like Listing 6.1. If you copy and paste the code, Android Studio will ask you if you want to import some classes. Select Yes. Basically, you need to modify Line 27, then add Lines 28-181.

Listing 6.1: TableView.java Class Code

```
1    package com.example.www.sampleapplication;
2
3    import android.app.ProgressDialog;
4    import android.content.Context;
5    import android.content.SharedPreferences;
6    import android.database.Cursor;
7    import android.net.Uri;
8    import android.os.Bundle;
9    import android.support.annotation.Nullable;
10   import
     android.support.v4.content.res.ResourcesCompat;
11   import
     android.support.v7.app.AppCompatActivity;
12   import android.util.Log;
13   import android.view.Gravity;
14   import android.view.ViewGroup;
15   import android.widget.ImageView;
16   import android.widget.RelativeLayout;
17   import android.widget.TableLayout;
18   import android.widget.TableRow;
19   import android.widget.TextView;
20
21   import java.util.ArrayList;
22   import java.util.Arrays;
23
24   /**
25    * Created by MIMA on 7/2/16.
26    */
27   public class TableView extends
     AppCompatActivity implements
```

```java
    LoadingTask.LoadingTaskFinishedListener {
28      String authority;
29      String path;
30      char request;
31      TableLayout tableLayout;
32      private static final String TAG =
    "TableView";
33      ProgressDialog PD;
34
35      @Override
36      protected void onCreate(@Nullable Bundle
    savedInstanceState) {
37          super.onCreate(savedInstanceState);
38          PD = new
    ProgressDialog(TableView.this);
39          Uri data = getIntent().getData();
40          authority = data.getAuthority();
41          path = data.getLastPathSegment();
42
43          if(authority.equalsIgnoreCase("open-
    figure")) {
44
    setContentView(R.layout.fragment_table_view);
45          } else {
46
    setContentView(R.layout.activity_table_view);
47              tableLayout = (TableLayout)
    findViewById(R.id.table_layout);
48          }
49
50          PD.setTitle("Please wait");
51          PD.setMessage("Loading...");
52          PD.setCancelable(false);
53          PD.show();
54
55          if(authority.equalsIgnoreCase("open-
    table")) {
56              this.request =
    LoadingTask.REQUEST_TABLE;
57              new LoadingTask(this,
    TableView.this, path).execute();
58          } else
```

```
59    if(authority.equalsIgnoreCase("open-box")) {
              this.request =
      LoadingTask.REQUEST_BOX;
60            new LoadingTask(this,
      TableView.this, path, this.request).execute();
61          } else
      if(authority.equalsIgnoreCase("open-footnote"))
      {
62            this.request =
      LoadingTask.REQUEST_FOOTNOTE;
63            new LoadingTask(this,
      TableView.this, path, this.request).execute();
64          } else
      if(authority.equalsIgnoreCase("open-figure")) {
65            this.request =
      LoadingTask.REQUEST_FIGURE;
66          } else {
67            badRequest(authority, path);
68          }
69        }
70
71      @Override
72      protected void onResume() {
73          super.onResume();
74          if(this.request ==
      LoadingTask.REQUEST_FIGURE) {
75              loadFigure(this.path);
76          }
77          if(PD.isShowing()) PD.dismiss();
78      }
79
80      private void loadFigure(String figName) {
81          String[] figs =
      getResources().getStringArray(R.array.encoded_l
      ist_of_figures);
82          ArrayList<String> list = new
      ArrayList<String>(Arrays.asList(figs));
83          if(!list.contains(path)) {
84              /* bad request for a figure name.
      bail out. */
85              TextView txt = new TextView(this);
86              txt.setLayoutParams(new
```

```java
87          TableRow.LayoutParams(ViewGroup.LayoutParams.WR
            AP_CONTENT,

            ViewGroup.LayoutParams.WRAP_CONTENT));
88              txt.setPadding(5, 5, 5, 5);
89              txt.setGravity(Gravity.CENTER);
90              txt.setText("Bad request for figure
            '" + figName + "'");
91              RelativeLayout relativeLayout =
            (RelativeLayout)
92          findViewById(R.id.table_relative_layout);
93              relativeLayout.addView(txt);
94              return;
95          }
96

            ImageView imageView =
            (ImageView)findViewById(R.id.image_view_area);
97          String PackageName =
            getApplicationContext().getPackageName();
98          Log.d(TAG, figName);
99
            imageView.setImageDrawable(ResourcesCompat.getD
            rawable(getResources(),
100
            getResources().getIdentifier("drawable/" +
            figName, "drawable", PackageName), null));
101         }
102
103     private void badRequest(String authority,
            String path) {
104         TableRow head = new TableRow(this);
105         head.setLayoutParams(new
            TableRow.LayoutParams(ViewGroup.LayoutParams.MA
            TCH_PARENT,
106
            android.app.ActionBar.LayoutParams.WRAP_CONTENT
            ));
107         head.setGravity(Gravity.CENTER);
108         TextView txt = new TextView(this);
109         txt.setLayoutParams(new
            TableRow.LayoutParams(ViewGroup.LayoutParams.WR
            AP_CONTENT,
```

```
110
   ViewGroup.LayoutParams.WRAP_CONTENT));
111        txt.setPadding(5, 5, 5, 5);
112        txt.setGravity(Gravity.CENTER);
113        txt.setText("Bad request '" + authority
   + "' for item '" + path + "'");
114        head.addView(txt);
115        tableLayout.addView(head);
116    }
117
118    @Override
119    public void onTaskFinished(Cursor cursor) {
120        if(this.request ==
   LoadingTask.REQUEST_TABLE) {
121
   getSupportActionBar().setSubtitle("Table
   View");
122            int rows = cursor.getCount();
123            int cols = cursor.getColumnCount();
124            Log.d(TAG, "cols = " + cols + ",
   rows = " + rows);
125            /* first add column heads */
126            TableRow head = new TableRow(this);
127            head.setLayoutParams(new
   TableRow.LayoutParams(ViewGroup.LayoutParams.MA
   TCH_PARENT,
128
   android.app.ActionBar.LayoutParams.WRAP_CONTENT
   ));
129            //head.setGravity(Gravity.CENTER);
130            for(int j = 1; j < cols; j++) {
   //skip the _ID column
131                TextView txt = new
   TextView(this);
132                txt.setLayoutParams(new
   TableRow.LayoutParams(ViewGroup.LayoutParams.WR
   AP_CONTENT,
133
   ViewGroup.LayoutParams.WRAP_CONTENT));
134                txt.setPadding(5, 5, 5, 5);
135
   txt.setBackgroundResource(R.drawable.cell_shape
```

```
);
136
            txt.setText(cursor.getColumnName(j));
137                 head.addView(txt);
138             }
139             tableLayout.addView(head);
140
141             cursor.moveToFirst();
142             for(int i = 0; i < rows; i++) {
143                 TableRow row = new
        TableRow(this);
144                 row.setLayoutParams(new
        TableRow.LayoutParams(ViewGroup.LayoutParams.MA
        TCH_PARENT,
145
        android.app.ActionBar.LayoutParams.WRAP_CONTENT
        ));
146
        //row.setGravity(Gravity.CENTER);
147                 for(int j = 1; j < cols; j++) {
        //skip the _ID column
148                     TextView txt = new
        TextView(this);
149                     txt.setLayoutParams(new
        TableRow.LayoutParams(ViewGroup.LayoutParams.WR
        AP_CONTENT,
150
        ViewGroup.LayoutParams.WRAP_CONTENT));
151                     txt.setPadding(5, 5, 5, 5);
152
        txt.setBackgroundResource(R.drawable.cell_shape
153     );

        txt.setText(cursor.getString(j));
154                     Log.d(TAG, i + ", " + j +
        ": " + cursor.getString(j));
155
156                     row.addView(txt);
157                 }
158                 cursor.moveToNext();
159                 tableLayout.addView(row);
            }
```

```
160        } else if(this.request ==
     LoadingTask.REQUEST_BOX ||
161              this.request ==
     LoadingTask.REQUEST_FOOTNOTE) {
162          if(this.request ==
     LoadingTask.REQUEST_BOX)
163
     getSupportActionBar().setSubtitle("SideBox
     View");
164          else
     getSupportActionBar().setSubtitle("Footnote
     View");
165          cursor.moveToFirst();
166          TableRow row = new TableRow(this);
167          row.setLayoutParams(new
     TableRow.LayoutParams(ViewGroup.LayoutParams.MA
     TCH_PARENT,
168
     android.app.ActionBar.LayoutParams.WRAP_CONTENT
     ));
169          row.setGravity(Gravity.CENTER);
170
171          TextView txt = new TextView(this);
172          txt.setLayoutParams(new
     TableRow.LayoutParams(ViewGroup.LayoutParams.WR
     AP_CONTENT,
173
     ViewGroup.LayoutParams.WRAP_CONTENT));
174          txt.setPadding(5, 5, 5, 5);
175
     txt.setText(cursor.getString(cursor.getColumnIn
     dexOrThrow("BodyText")));
176          row.addView(txt);
177          tableLayout.addView(row);
178        }
179      if(PD.isShowing()) PD.dismiss();
180    }
181 }
```

Here is what the code in Listing 6.1 does:
- Line 27: declare this class as a descendant of

AppCompatActivity, which means it is an activity. Also, this class implements the LoadingTaskFinishedListener interface which we need in order to communicate with the LoadingTask class.

- Lines 28-29: here we will save the URI's **authority** and **path**. In our case, the authority would be a request string, such as "open-table", "open-figure", "open-footnote", or "open-box", which in effect indicates what we are requested to open, so that we will query the correct database table. The path would tell us which table, figure, footnote, or box we actually need to display.

- Line 30: convert the string **authority** into a simple integer value, the values of which were defined in LoadingTask class (lines 20-23 of Listing 5.3).

- Line 31: the table layout we will use as a container to view tables, footnote and side-boxes. We will define it in the layout view later.

- Line 32: tag required by the debugger for logging debug messages.

- Line 33: a progress dialog we will show to the user while we are loading from the database.

- Line 36: this is the function that Android system will call whenever it creates a new instance of this activity.

- Line 37: always call the parent's `onCreate()` function.

- Line 38: create a progress dialog.

- Lines 39-41: get the URI data that is packaged in the Intent that was sent to us. Extract from it the authority and path fields.

- Lines 43-48: tell the system what layout to use as the UI of this activity, according to whether we are going to view a figure or text. The layouts are showed in red in the Studio because we haven't defined them yet.

- Lines 50-53: set progress dialog's title and body message, then show it to the user.

- Lines 55-68: according to the request (as defined by the **authority** part of the URI) we will save what request what it, then start a new instance of LoadingTask and pass it the information on what to load. It will do the job of loading from the database in the background, and when it finishes it will call our `onTaskFinished()` function, which we define in line 119. In case we couldn't figure out what requested is it, we call the `badRequest()` function, which is defined on line 103, to display an error message.

- Lines 72-78: this function is called by the Android system after the activity is visible and just before it becomes reactive to the user. We use it to load the requested figure, in case the request was to load a figure. Otherwise, it just dismisses the progress dialog.

- Line 80: if the request was to view a figure, this function does the work of fetching and loading it to view.

- Lines 81-82: when **dbprep** parsed our book earlier on, it created two lists of figures: one contains the actual names of figures as they appear in the TOC, and a second list of "encoded" figure names, which refers to the file names of figures, which are usually too ugly to be seen by the user. This is why we show the user the **list_of_figures** string array from **strings.xml** file, while internally we use the **encoded_list_of_figures** to access figure files.

- Lines 83-94: check if the **encoded_list_of_figures** string array contains the request **path**, i.e. if the requested figure name is actually in the list. If not, create a new TextView and set it's text as an error message indicating that the figure was not found, and add it to the view. The **R.id.table_relative_layout** on line 91 is not defined yet, we will define it later.

- Lines 96-100: if the figure is indeed listed, load the figure into the ImageView named **R.id.image_view_area** that we will define later.

- Lines 103-116: if the request is not understood, i.e. for some reason it so happened that another application knew how to call us and summoned this activity with a malformed request, we should die gracefully instead of crashing. This function provides a decent error message that will be shown on the view to tell the user something went wrong.

- Line 119: this is the callback function that LoadingTask will call when it finishes loading from the database. The result of database query is returned to us in a Cursor that we will use to view the result rows.

- Line 120: check if the request was to view a table.
- Line 121: if so, set the subtitle to indicate we are viewing a table.
- Lines 122-123: get the count of rows and columns in the result.
- Line 124: just a debug message.
- Lines 126-129: create a new table row to add the names of the columns to it.
- Lines 130-138: iterate through the column names, skipping the first column with the name **_id** as it is an internal column and the user will not benefit from seeing it. Add each column name to the first row of our table.
- Line 139: add the header row to the table.
- Lines 141-159: move to the first row of the results. Iterate through the data, row by row, adding cells to each row, column by column. Move to the next row and repeat until the rows are all added to the table view.
- Lines 160-178: if the request is to view a footnote or a side-box, things are easier. Here we would have only one row, so we would create a single table row with a single cell that we will fill with the **BodyText** field of the result.
- Line 179: if the progress dialog is still showing, dismiss it.

There are some red items on the class view that we will need to remedy. We are going to do these things in the following sections.

6.3 Adding the activity_table_view Layout

In the Project Navigation pane on the left, double click on **res**. Right click on **layout,** and select **New → Layout Resource File**. In the **New Resource File** dialog box, add the following:

- File name: **activity_table_view**
- Root element: **LinearLayout**
- Source set: **main**

- Directory name: **layout**

Then click **OK**. The layout file is added and is opened for editing in the Design view. Change the AppTheme to DeviceDefault.Light, and then switch to Text view. The XML file should look like:

```
<?xml version="1.0" encoding="utf-8"?>
<LinearLayout
xmlns:android="http://schemas.android.com/apk/res/and
roid"
    android:orientation="vertical"
android:layout_width="match_parent"
    android:layout_height="match_parent">

</LinearLayout>
```

Edit the file to look like Listing 6.2. We would usually edit layouts in the *Design* mode, but in this case, it would be easier and quicker to edit (or copy and paste) the XML code directly.

Listing 6.2: activity_table_view.xml File

```
1   <?xml version="1.0" encoding="utf-8"?>
2   <LinearLayout
    xmlns:android="http://schemas.android.com/apk/re
    s/android"
3       android:layout_width="match_parent"
4       android:layout_height="match_parent"
5       android:id="@+id/table_linear_layout"
6       android:orientation="vertical">
7
8       <HorizontalScrollView
9           android:layout_width="wrap_content"
10          android:layout_height="match_parent"
11          android:layout_gravity="center"
12          android:id="@+id/horizontalScrollView2"
    >
13
14          <ScrollView
    android:layout_height="wrap_content"
15
    xmlns:android="http://schemas.android.com/apk/re
```

```
16        s/android"
17                android:layout_width="wrap_content"
18                android:id="@+id/table_scroll_view">
19
20            <TableLayout
       xmlns:android="http://schemas.android.com/apk/re
       s/android"
21     android:layout_width="match_parent"

22     android:layout_height="wrap_content"
23                android:id="@+id/table_layout"
                   android:gravity="top|
       center_horizontal">
24            </TableLayout>
25
26        </ScrollView>
27     </HorizontalScrollView>
28
29  </LinearLayout>
```

This is the layout we will use when we are displaying a table, a footnote or a side-box. We create a HorizontalScrollView to enable horizontal scrolling. Inside it we create a ScrollView to enable vertical scrolling. Inside it we create a TableView in which we will add TextViews in the TableView activity to display the target text.

6.4 Adding the fragment_table_view Layout

In the Project Navigation pane on the left, double click on **res**. Right click on **layout,** and select **New → Layout Resource File**. In the **New Resource File** dialog box, add the following:

- File name: **fragment_table_view**
- Root element: **RelativeLayout**
- Source set: **main**
- Directory name: **layout**

Then click **OK**. The layout file is added and is opened for editing in the Design view. Change the AppTheme to DeviceDefault.Light, and then switch to Text view. The XML file should look like:

```
<?xml version="1.0" encoding="utf-8"?>
<RelativeLayout
xmlns:android="http://schemas.android.com/apk/res/and
roid"
    android:layout_width="match_parent"
android:layout_height="match_parent">


</RelativeLayout>
```

Edit the file to look like Listing 6.3. We would usually edit layouts in the *Design* mode, but in this case, it would be easier and quicker to edit (or copy and paste) the XML code directly.

Listing 6.3: fragment_table_view.xml File

```
1   <?xml version="1.0" encoding="utf-8"?>
2   <RelativeLayout
    xmlns:android="http://schemas.android.com/apk/res
    /android"
3       android:orientation="vertical"
    android:layout_width="match_parent"
4       android:layout_height="match_parent"
5       android:id="@+id/table_relative_layout">
6
7       <ScrollView
8           android:layout_width="wrap_content"
9           android:layout_height="match_parent"
10          android:id="@+id/scrollView2" >
11
12          <HorizontalScrollView
13              android:layout_width="wrap_content"
14              android:layout_height="wrap_content"
15
    android:id="@+id/horizontalScrollView" >
16
17              <ImageView
18
    android:layout_width="wrap_content"
19
    android:layout_height="wrap_content"
```

```
20                  android:id="@+id/image_view_area"
     />
21          </HorizontalScrollView>
22      </ScrollView>
23
24  </RelativeLayout>
```

This is the layout we will use when we are displaying a figure. We create a ScrollView to enable vertical scrolling. Inside it we create a HorizontalScrollView to enable horizontal scrolling. Inside it we create an ImageView in which we load the target figure in the TableView activity.

6.5 Adding the cell_shape Drawable

We need our tables to have solid borders. In order to do this, we need to define a drawable object that we will use as cells' background.
In the Project Navigation pane on the left, double click on **res**. Right click on **drawable,** and select **New → Drawable Resource File**. In the **New Resource File** dialog box, add the following:

- File name: **cell_shape**
- Source set: **main**
- Directory name: **drawable**

Then click **OK**. The drawable file is added and is opened for editing. The XML file should look like:

```
<?xml version="1.0" encoding="utf-8"?>
<selector
xmlns:android="http://schemas.android.com/apk/res/and
roid">

</selector>
```

Edit the file to look like Listing 6.4.

Listing 6.4: cell_shape.xml File

```
1   <?xml version="1.0" encoding="utf-8"?>
2       <shape
```

```
3    xmlns:android="http://schemas.android.com/apk/res
     /android"
4          android:shape= "rectangle"  >
5          <solid android:color="#00ffffff"/>
6          <stroke android:width="1dp"
     android:color="#000000"/>
7        </shape>
```

The drawable XML file defines a rectangular shape with a white background and a black border with a width of 1 pixel.

6.6 Editing the LoadingTask Class

Currently our LoadingTask class can only load chapter sections from the database. We need to extend it to load tables, footnotes and side-boxes.

Open the **LoadingTask.java** class file. Go to the end of line 16 which reads:

```
private ReadingActivity parentRA;
```

Press ENTER to open a new line, and write:

```
private TableView parentTV;
```

Now go to line 41 (empty line after the end of LoadingTask constructor). Add:

```
    public LoadingTask(LoadingTaskFinishedListener
finishedListener, TableView parent,
                    String table) {
        this.finishedListener = finishedListener;
        this.table = table;
        this.parentTV = parent;
        this.myContext = parent.getBaseContext();
        this.request = REQUEST_TABLE;
    }

    public LoadingTask(LoadingTaskFinishedListener
```

```
finishedListener, TableView parent,
        String boxOrFootnote, char request) {
    this.finishedListener = finishedListener;
    this.boxOrFootnote = boxOrFootnote;
    this.parentTV = parent;
    this.myContext = parent.getBaseContext();
    this.request = request;
}
```

Now our LoadingTask class is capable of loading tables, footnotes and side-boxes.

6.7 Editing AndroidManifest.xml

In order for the Android system to be able to see our TableView activity and launch it, we need to declare it in the manifest file. Open AndoidManifest.xml, go to line 25 (empty line just after the </activity> closing tag of ReadingActivity) and write:

```
<activity android:name=".TableView">
    <intent-filter>
        <category android:name=
"android.intent.category.DEFAULT" />
        <action android:name=
"android.intent.action.VIEW" />
        <data android:scheme=
"com.example.www.sampleapplication" />
    </intent-filter>
</activity>
```

This declares the TableView activity in order to be recognized by the Android system. It tells that our activity can receive intents with ACTION_VIEW action, which have a URI with the scheme set to our package name. This makes sure we don't receive intents that are requesting ACTION_VIEW for other types of data, like web pages, images and so on.

6.8 Editing the MainMenuFragment Class

Remember that in our main TOC, we have three entries: list of tables, list of figures, and list of boxes?. But the three of them are not working. We need to enable them in the MainMenuFragment class. Open **MainMenuFragment.java** and go to line 102 where it says:

```
} else if(this.whoAmI == LIST_SUB_MENU) {
    /* To be done later */
} else {
```

Remove the commented line (line 103) and insert:

```
1    String query;
2    String whatToDo;
3    String itemName;
4    if(this.menuIndex == LIST_OF_TABLES) {
5            whatToDo = "open-table";
6            itemName = "table" + position;
7    } else if(this.menuIndex == LIST_OF_FIGURES) {
8            whatToDo = "open-figure";
9            String[] figs =
     getResources().getStringArray(R.array.encoded_li
     st_of_figures);
10           itemName = figs[position];
11   } else if(this.menuIndex == LIST_OF_BOXES) {
12           whatToDo = "open-box";
13           itemName = "box" + position;
14   } else {
15           whatToDo = "";
16           itemName = "";
17   }
18   query = PackageName + "://" + whatToDo + "/" +
     itemName;
19   Uri link = Uri.parse(query);
20   Intent myIntent = new Intent(Intent.ACTION_VIEW,
     link);
21   startActivity(myIntent);
```

What the codes does is that it constructs a URI according to the required item, whether it was a table, a figure or a side-box. The resultant URI would be, for example, if we wanted to view the first table, which is table #0:

```
com.example.www.sampleapplication://open-table/table0
```

Then the TableView class will do the rest to fetch the data and display it.

Now your App is almost ready. Go around and try it out. Click on some menu items. Open up a section and click on a table link. Click the Back button and try something else.
You will notice that if you click on a figure's link, the application will crash, as we didn't copy the figures to the App's folder yet. We will do this next.

6.9 Adding Your Figure Files to the App

I assume that you either have your book's figures as separate files, or you extracted them from your manuscript as I showed you in section "3.6 Final Notes Before You Go".
You need to copy those figure files into the App's resources. But before doing that, we must make sure that your files follow the rules we set out in section "3.4.3 Figure Naming Rules".
If your files are numerous and you are not sure that you followed the rules for all of them, there is a tool to help you.
I wrote a small C program for this purpose: fixing figure file names to follow the rules. You can download the executable for GNU/Linux from:
http://sites.google.com/site/mohammedisam2000/android-app-ebook/fixfigs
Or, otherwise, download the source (one C source file) from:
http://sites.google.com/site/mohammedisam2000/android-app-ebook/fixfigs.c, and compile it.

Now open a terminal. Change directory to where you downloaded the executable, and invoke it:

```
./fixfigs
```

The tool needs you to tell it the folder where you have your figures. This is why it will show you this message:

```
[MIMA@localhost dbprep]$ ./fixfigs
Extra or missing argument(s). Invoke me as:
  ./fixfigs input-dir
Where:
  input-dir:  directory where your book figure files
reside
[MIMA@localhost dbprep]$
```

Now copy all your figure files into one folder. Invoke the tool with the name of the folder, say:

```
./fixfigs folder-name
```

You should see a series of output lines showing what files the tool found, and if it fixed any of them, along with any errors encountered. Review the output as it is self-explanatory and will help you to understand what's happening.

Now open this folder in your file browser. Select all the figure files (CTRL+A usually does the trick), then copy them (CTRL+C on most file browsers). Navigate to your project's folder. Open **app** → **src** → **main** → **res** → **drawable**, and paste all the files there (CTRL+V). Now your files should be discovered by the Android Studio. You can check this by going to the Project Navigation pane, double click on **res,** then double click on **drawable**. You should see a list corresponding to your figure files.

Your eBook is now fully-functional. If you want to deploy it now, you are free to. Just make sure you test it thoroughly, by yourself and by giving it to close friends or family to test-drive it. Try your best to make it crash. Always assume there is some dumb user who will manage somehow to crash your app. Try to make it as clean as possible, so that your users will be happy with their experience. This is how you build a good reputation, promote your Apps, and gather the fruits of your effort.

In the next chapter we will add some extra features. While they are not mandatory for the functioning of your app, their presence will improve your Apps reviews and users will be very happy that you spent some extra effort and thought about implementing those features. So here we go.

Chaper 7: Perfecting Your Application

7.1 Saving Activity State

If you remember our talk on the Activity life-cycle, we said that the Activity can be stopped or paused. This happens when the user starts another activity that fully or partially obscures our activity, respectively. In both cases, our activity is alive. The system just keeps it in a safe place until the user navigates back to it, in which case the system takes out our activity instance from where it stored it, and restores everything to where the user left it. All partially-filled text boxes, selected list items, checked checkboxes, unfilled forms, and whatever changes the user has made would be recreated automatically by the system.

But then there is another situation. When the system needs to free memory for some other high priority task, it might need to kill our activity. Later on, the user decides to navigate back to our activity, but he doesn't know that the system has silently killed it. He expects the activity to open as when he left it. In that case, the system will need to create a new instance of the activity, and reconstruct everything so the user will never know what happened.

But the system can only save some things, like the state of the user interface components. Some other things cannot be saved by the system, notably your internal variables. Those you have to save yourself.

So when the system is about to put your activity in the background, where it *might* be destroyed later, it calls a special function, onSaveInstanceState(), so that you can save important information that you need to retrieve later.

Later, if the user navigates back to your activity after it being killed by the system, another function, onRestoreInstanceState(), is called, where you can reinstate your variables and retrieve state information you saved earlier.

Another thing happens when your activity starts another activity, as when the user selects an item from the TOC, and we fire an intent to launch a ReadingActivity or a TableView. When this happens, the system calls another function, onPause(), before calling yet another one, onStop(), before starting the new activity.

It is advisable to save permanent information, like writing data to a database, in one of those two functions. Keep in mind that onPause() is called *while* the new activity is being created, so if it does a long-running task, the user interface would be stalled or delayed. This is why onPause() must be kept short and quick.

In the next few sections we are going to make changes to our activities to make sure we save our state, so that when the user navigates back to our activity after being somewhere else, he starts right where he left us.

7.2 Editing the MainActivity Class

Open the **MainActivity.java** class file. Go to the end of line 6, where the declaration of the class is, and press ENTER. Add those lines:

```
public static final int CURRENT_ACTIVITY_NONE = 0;
public static final int CURRENT_ACTIVITY_MAIN = 1;
public static final int CURRENT_ACTIVITY_READING = 2;
public static final int CURRENT_ACTIVITY_TABLE_VIEW =
3;
```

Those constants define the different activities. When we are shutdown, each activity will write to the storage its number, so that when we come back, we know which activity was last open.

Now change onCreate() function to make it look like Listing 7.1.

Listing 7.1: onCreate() function in **MainActivity.java** Class

1	@Override
2	protected void onCreate(Bundle savedInstanceState) {
3	super.onCreate(savedInstanceState);
4	setContentView(R.layout.activity_main);
5	/* maybe we are returning after user pressed Back button? */

```
6      if(savedInstanceState != null) {
7          return;
8      }
9      SharedPreferences sPref =
10 this.getSharedPreferences(getString(R.string.pref
   erence_file), Context.MODE_PRIVATE);
11     int CurrentActivity =
   sPref.getInt("CurrentActivity",
   CURRENT_ACTIVITY_NONE);
12     if(CurrentActivity ==
   CURRENT_ACTIVITY_READING) {
13         Intent myIntent = new Intent();
14         myIntent.setClass(MainActivity.this,
   ReadingActivity.class);
15         startActivity(myIntent);
16         } else if(CurrentActivity ==
   CURRENT_ACTIVITY_TABLE_VIEW) {
17             String PackageName =
   getApplicationContext().getPackageName();
18             String authority =
   sPref.getString("authority", "");
19             String path = sPref.getString("path",
   "");
20             String query = PackageName + "://" +
   authority + "/" + path;
21             Intent myIntent = new Intent();
22             myIntent.setClass(MainActivity.this,
   TableView.class);
23             startActivity(myIntent);
24     }
25
26     MainMenuFragment menu = new
   MainMenuFragment();
27     if(CurrentActivity == CURRENT_ACTIVITY_MAIN)
   {
28         menu.whoAmI = sPref.getInt("whoAmI",
   MainMenuFragment.MAIN_MENU);
29         menu.menuIndex =
   sPref.getInt("menuIndex", 0);
30     } else {
31         menu.whoAmI = MainMenuFragment.MAIN_MENU;
```

```
32        }
33        android.app.FragmentTransaction transaction =
       getFragmentManager().beginTransaction();
34           transaction.replace(R.id.main_menu_container,
       menu);
35           transaction.commit();
36    }
```

The code does the following:

- Lines 6-8: when the activity is created, the system send a **Bundle** object to let us know about the previous state the activity was in. If this is the first time our activity is created, the object is NULL. In either case, if you implemented onRestoreInstanceState(), you don't need to use this object as the same object is passed to both functions by the system.

- Lines 9-10: we request the system to give us a reference to our shared preferences, which is stored by the system in our application's area in the internal storage. We pass the name of our preference file, a string resource we are going to create later.

- Line 11: preferences are saved as key-value pairs. We ask for an integer value, denoted by the string key "CurrentActivity". If the key string is not present in preferences, i.e. we didn't save state before, a default value of CURRENT_ACTIVITY_NONE is returned.

- Lines 12-15: if the last open activity was a ReadingActivity, create an intent to start it off.

- Lines 16-23: if the last open activity was a TableView, create a query stating what was open (table, footnote, figure or side-box) and an intent to start it off.

- Lines 27-31: if the last open activity was us, i.e. a MainActivity, try to find out which menu exactly was open. If there was none, start fresh as this is the first time the activity is created.

We need to add a string resource that names our preference file. Open the **strings.xml** file. Go to the end of the first line that reads:

144

\<resources\> and press ENTER. Add the following line:

```
<string
name="preference_file">com.example.www.sampleapplicat
ion.PREFERENCE_FILE</string>
```

This gives a unique name to our shared preferences file.

7.3 Editing the MainMenuFragment Class

Open the **MainMenuFragment.java** class file. Go to the end of onListItemClick() function (the closing curly brace on the line before-the-last), go to the end of the line (outside the function) and press ENTER. Add this function:

```
1      @Override
2      public void onPause() {
3          super.onPause();
4          if(getActivity().isFinishing()) {
5              SharedPreferences sPref =
6
       getActivity().getSharedPreferences(getString(R.st
       ring.preference_file), Context.MODE_PRIVATE);
7              SharedPreferences.Editor edit =
       sPref.edit();
8                  edit.putInt("CurrentActivity",
       MainActivity.CURRENT_ACTIVITY_MAIN);
9                  edit.putInt("whoAmI", whoAmI);
10                 edit.putInt("menuIndex", menuIndex);
11                 Log.d(TAG, "Saving (Act " +
       MainActivity.CURRENT_ACTIVITY_MAIN + ")");
12                 edit.commit();
13         }
14     }
```

This function is called when the activity is going to the background. It saves the important internal variables that we will need later to reopen the menu in the correct position.

7.4 Editing the ReadingActivity Class

Open the **ReadingActivity.java** class file. Fix onCreate() function to make it look like Listing 7.2.

Listing 7.2: onCreate() function in **ReadingActivity.java** Class

```
1       @Override
2       protected void onCreate(@Nullable Bundle
    savedInstanceState) {
3           super.onCreate(savedInstanceState);
4
    setContentView(R.layout.activity_reading);
5           PackageName =
    getApplicationContext().getPackageName();
6
7           /* maybe we are returning after user
    pressed Back button? */
8           if(savedInstanceState != null) {
9               return;
10          }
11          SharedPreferences sPref =
12
    this.getSharedPreferences(getString(R.string.pref
    erence_file), Context.MODE_PRIVATE);
13          int CurrentActivity =
    sPref.getInt("CurrentActivity",
    MainActivity.CURRENT_ACTIVITY_NONE);
14          Log.d(TAG, "Activ" + CurrentActivity);
15
16          if(CurrentActivity ==
    MainActivity.CURRENT_ACTIVITY_READING) {
17              chap = sPref.getInt("chap", 0);
18              section = sPref.getInt("section", 0);
19              Log.d(TAG, "Reading (C " + chap + ",
    S " + section + ")");
20          } else {
21              chap =
    getIntent().getIntExtra(PackageName + ".chap",
    0);
22              section =
    getIntent().getIntExtra(PackageName + ".section",
    0);
```

```
23              }
24
25          PD = new
    ProgressDialog(ReadingActivity.this);
26          PD.setTitle("Please wait");
27          PD.setMessage("Loading...");
28          PD.setCancelable(false);
29          PD.show();
30          setSubTitle();
31          sectionNumView =
    (TextView)findViewById(R.id.reading_section_numbe
    r);
32          chapNameView =
    (Spinner)findViewById(R.id.reading_chap_name_list
    );
33
34          /* set the event handler for the Chapters
    drop-down list */
35
    chapNameView.setOnItemSelectedListener(new
    AdapterView.OnItemSelectedListener() {
36              @Override
37              public void
    onItemSelected(AdapterView<?> adapterView, View
    view, int i, long l) {
38                  PD.show();
39                  section = i;
40                  new
    LoadingTask(ReadingActivity.this,
    ReadingActivity.this, chap, section).execute();
41              }
42
43              @Override
44              public void
    onNothingSelected(AdapterView<?> adapterView) {
45
46              }
47          });
48          getSectionNames(this.section);
49      }
```

The function checks to see if there are saved preferences. If so, it checks to see if the last saved activity was us, i.e. a ReadingActivity. If so, it loads the chapter and section numbers from preferences. Otherwise, we are called from the main menu, and we read this information from the coming intent.

Now go to the end of the file, just after the end of getSectionNames() function. Open a new line *after* the end of the function and insert the functions in Listing 7.3.

Listing 7.3: Functions onSaveInstanceState(), onRestoreInstanceState() and onPause() of **ReadingActivity.java** Class

```
1        @Override
2        protected void onSaveInstanceState(Bundle
    outState) {
3            outState.putInt("chap", chap);
4            outState.putInt("section", section);
5            outState.putInt("sectionCount",
    sectionCount);
6            /* call the superclass so it can save the
    view hierarchy state */
7            super.onSaveInstanceState(outState);
8        }
9
10       @Override
11       protected void onRestoreInstanceState(Bundle
    savedInstanceState) {
12           /* call the superclass so it can restore
    the view hierarchy */
13
    super.onRestoreInstanceState(savedInstanceState);
14           /* Restore state members from saved
    instance */
15           chap = savedInstanceState.getInt("chap");
16           section =
    savedInstanceState.getInt("section");
17           sectionCount =
    savedInstanceState.getInt("sectionCount");
18       }
19
20       @Override
```

148

```
21      protected void onPause() {
22          super.onPause();
23          SharedPreferences sPref =
24
    this.getSharedPreferences(getString(R.string.pref
    erence_file), Context.MODE_PRIVATE);
25          SharedPreferences.Editor edit =
    sPref.edit();
26          /* if finishing, we are going back to
    papa, MainActivity */
27          if(isFinishing()) {
28              edit.putInt("CurrentActivity",
    MainActivity.CURRENT_ACTIVITY_MAIN);
29              Log.d(TAG, "I am finishing");
30          } else {
31              edit.putInt("CurrentActivity",
    MainActivity.CURRENT_ACTIVITY_READING);
32              edit.putInt("chap", chap);
33              edit.putInt("section", section);
34          }
35          Log.d(TAG, "Saving (C " + chap + ", S " +
    section + ")");
36          edit.commit();
37      }
```

7.5 Editing the TableView Class

Open the **TableView.java** class file. Fix onCreate() function to make it look like Listing 7.4.

Listing 7.4: onCreate() function in **TableView.java** Class

```
1       @Override
2       protected void onCreate(@Nullable Bundle
    savedInstanceState) {
3           super.onCreate(savedInstanceState);
4           PD = new ProgressDialog(TableView.this);
5
6           SharedPreferences sPref =
7
```

```
this.getSharedPreferences(getString(R.string.pref
erence_file), Context.MODE_PRIVATE);
        int CurrentActivity =
sPref.getInt("CurrentActivity",
MainActivity.CURRENT_ACTIVITY_NONE);
        Log.d(TAG, "Activ " + CurrentActivity);
        if(CurrentActivity ==
MainActivity.CURRENT_ACTIVITY_TABLE_VIEW) {
            authority =
sPref.getString("authority", "");
            path = sPref.getString("path", "");
        } else {
            Uri data = getIntent().getData();
            authority = data.getAuthority();
            path = data.getLastPathSegment();
        }

        if(authority.equalsIgnoreCase("open-
figure")) {

setContentView(R.layout.fragment_table_view);
        } else {

setContentView(R.layout.activity_table_view);
            tableLayout = (TableLayout)
findViewById(R.id.table_layout);
        }

        PD.setTitle("Please wait");
        PD.setMessage("Loading...");
        PD.setCancelable(false);
        PD.show();

        if(authority.equalsIgnoreCase("open-
table")) {
            this.request =
LoadingTask.REQUEST_TABLE;
            new LoadingTask(this, TableView.this,
path).execute();
        } else
if(authority.equalsIgnoreCase("open-box")) {
            this.request =
```

```
                LoadingTask.REQUEST_BOX;
36                  new LoadingTask(this, TableView.this,
                path, this.request).execute();
37                } else
                if(authority.equalsIgnoreCase("open-footnote")) {
38                  this.request =
                LoadingTask.REQUEST_FOOTNOTE;
39                  new LoadingTask(this, TableView.this,
                path, this.request).execute();
40                } else
                if(authority.equalsIgnoreCase("open-figure")) {
41                  this.request =
                LoadingTask.REQUEST_FIGURE;
42                } else {
43                  badRequest(authority, path);
44                }
45            }
```

Now to go the end of the file, just after the end of onTaskFinished() function. Open a new line *after* the end of the function and insert the functions in Listing 7.5.

Listing 7.5: Function onPause() of **TableView.java** Class

```
1       @Override
2       protected void onPause() {
3           super.onPause();
4           SharedPreferences sPref =
5
        this.getSharedPreferences(getString(R.string.pref
        erence_file), Context.MODE_PRIVATE);
6           SharedPreferences.Editor edit =
        sPref.edit();
7           /* if finishing, we are going back to
        papa, MainActivity */
8           if(isFinishing()) {
9               edit.putInt("CurrentActivity",
        MainActivity.CURRENT_ACTIVITY_MAIN);
10              Log.d(TAG, "I am finishing");
11          } else {
12              edit.putInt("CurrentActivity",
        MainActivity.CURRENT_ACTIVITY_TABLE_VIEW);
```

```
13          edit.putString("authority",
     authority);
14          edit.putString("path", path);
15      }
16      Log.d(TAG, "Saving (Auth " + authority +
     ", path " + path + ")");
17      edit.commit();
18  }
```

Now try out those changes. Open the application in AVD, open a table or a section, then navigate away. You can do this by pressing the Home button, or by selecting another activity from the Recent activities menu. Then go to the launcher and start the application. It should get you right were you left. Cool, right?.

7.6 Editing Your App's Launcher Icon

So far, we have been using the default App launcher icon, which Android Studio provides. You will most probably want to change this to your custom icon.

There is a lot to be said about designing good graphics and paying attention to the differing screen sizes and densities that your App might run on. We are not going into those details here. Instead, we will use a simple way to get your app it's custom made icon.

Open your project's folder in the file browser, then open **app → src → main → res**. You will find five **mipmap** folders:

- mipmap-hdpi
- mipmap-mdpi
- mipmap-xhdpi
- mipmap-xxhdpi
- mipmap-xxxhdpi

In each of these folders, you will find a file named **ic_launcher.png,** which shows the infamous Android green head. If you open those files with a viewer that shows you image size (like **Image Viewer** or **Shotwell Viewer** under GNU/Linux) you will see that those files, although seemingly bearing the same image, in fact have different sizes:

- ic_launcher.png in mipmap-hdpi: 72 x 72 pixels
- ic_launcher.png in mipmap-mdpi: 48 x 48 pixels
- ic_launcher.png in mipmap-xhdpi: 96 x 96 pixels
- ic_launcher.png in mipmap-xxhdpi: 144 x 144 pixels
- ic_launcher.png in mipmap-xxxhdpi: 192 x 192 pixels

I would suggest you start by editing the highest density icon, the one in the **mipmap-xxxhdpi** (with 3 X's) folder. Open it in a simple bitmap editor. If you are using Windows, MS Paint is a simple enough choice. If you are using GNU/Linux, you can use **KolourPaint** (http://www.kolourpaint.org). Of course, if you are comfortable using more sophisticated software like Adobe Photoshop or the GIMP, you are free to use any.

Now before editing the icon file I would suggest making a copy in the same folder, in case you made some mistake and wanted to start over. Don't mix files from different folders as those bear the same name but are quite different beasts.

Open the icon file in your image editor. Wipe out the whole canvas, and draw your image. Save this file and close it. Remember, this is the **ic_launcher.png** from the **mipmap-xxxhdpi** folder.

Now we need to resize this file to fit the different densities. If you have a good way you know to do this, do it. For those of you who don't know how to do it, here is a simple method.

Open the file you just closed using GIMP (GNU Image Manipulation Program, https://www.gimp.org/downloads/). From the menu, select **Image → Scale Image...** The dialog box in Figure 7.1 shows up.

We want to resize the image to fit the xxhdpi size (144 x 144 pixels). In the Width and Height fields, enter 144 in each. Click **Scale**. You will see the image is scaled to a smaller size.

Now select **File → Export As**, or press CTRL+SHIFT+E. Navigate to the **mipmap-xxhdpi** folder, and select the **ic_launcher.png** file. The GIMP will ask you to confirm that you want to overwrite the existing file, press Yes.

Now undo the scaling you did. Select **Edit → Undo,** or press **CTRL+Z**. The image is now at the size it was in when we started.

Now resize the image to fit the xhdpi size (96 x 96 pixels). Select

Image → Scale Image... and enter 96 in the Width and Height fields and click **Scale**. Select **File → Export As**, and navigate to the **mipmap-xhdpi** folder, and select the **ic_launcher.png** file. The GIMP will ask you to confirm that you want to overwrite the existing file, press Yes.

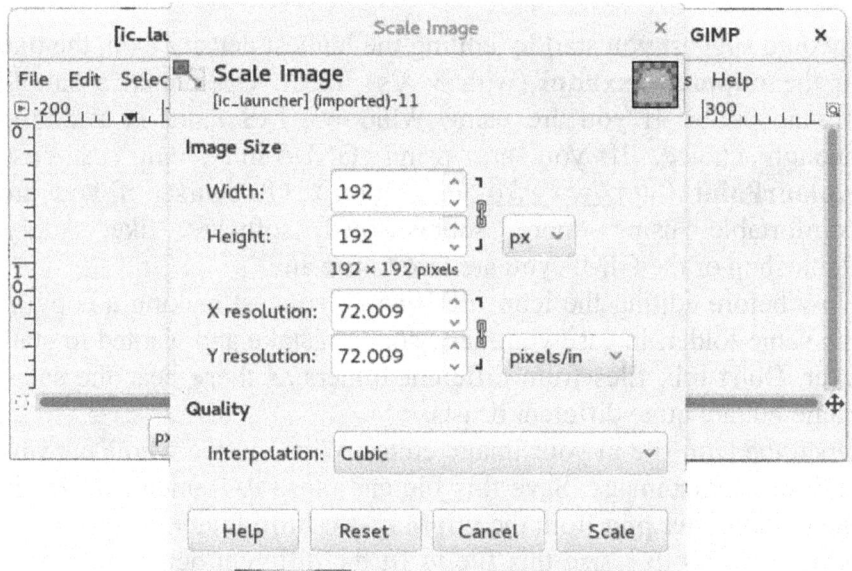

Figure 7.1: The **Scale Image** Dialog Box.

Undo that scaling. Rescale again to fit the mdpi and hdpi sizes and save those in the respective folders using the same process above. When finished, close the GIMP.

Now you have an icon that fits different screen densities. To make this stick to your app, you need to uninstall the app manually from the AVD, then re-run it from the Android Studio. Now your app is showing your custom icon.

7.7 More Things To Do

Some of the additional features that you can add to your App to make it more user-friendly:

- Add a Search button to help users search for content in your App.
- Add a Bookmarks button to allow users to save their bookmarks in your App's database.
- Change colors, images, backgrounds and the theme of your App.
- Extend the TableView class to enable the user to zoom in/out images, and change the text size.

Chapter 8: Publishing Your App

8.1 Generating an Application Package (APK) File

In order to publish your App, you need to prepare it in the form of an APK. This APK is the file you will distribute to the Google Play Store and to your users so that they can install and run your App.

Open your application in the Android Studio. Select from the menu: **Build → Generate Signed APK.** The dialog box in Figure 8.1 shows up.

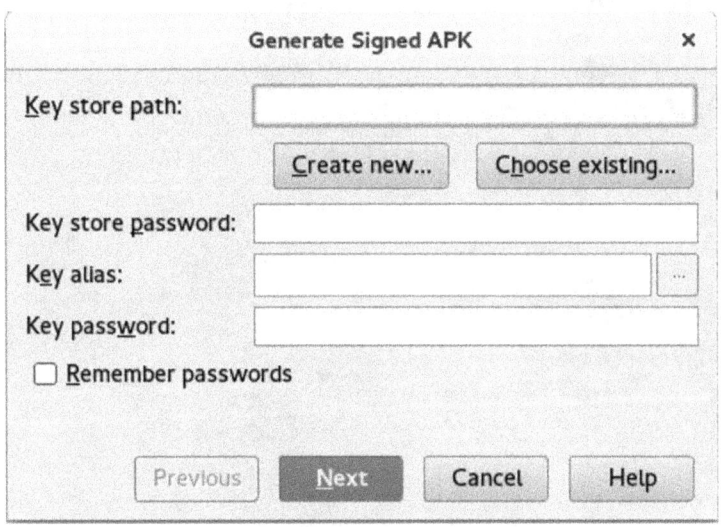

Figure 8.1: Generate Signed APK Dialog Box.

All Android applications must be digitally signed, at least to make sure we know who is the owner of the application. Your digital signature certificates are saved in a special file called the *keystore*. Certificates are pairs of public and private keys. The private key is kept in a safe place by the App developer, the public key is the distributable key.

If this is the first time your create a keystore, click the **Create New..** button. You will need to select a file to create as the new keystore file. You will also provide a password to guard the keystore. Then you will create a key, giving another password to guard the key, and an alias (a name) for that key. The key expires after the Validity field in years, which is 25 years by default. Keep it that way. You will then fill your personal details in the rest of the form, of which you need to provide at least one. Click OK. This will create a file with the extension **.jks** in the path you specified.

If you already created a keystore before, click the **Choose Existing...** button and select your keystore file.

Enter the keystore password. Select a key alias and enter the password for that key. Click **Next**.

In the next screen, select the path where you want the APK file to be generated. From the **Build Type** drop-down list, select **release**. Click **Finish**.

Sit back and wait while the Gradle build system builds the APK. After it finishes, it will show you a message on the top-right corner of the Android Studio window, as shown in Figure 8.2. Click on the **Show in File Manager** link to open the folder in which your APK is created.

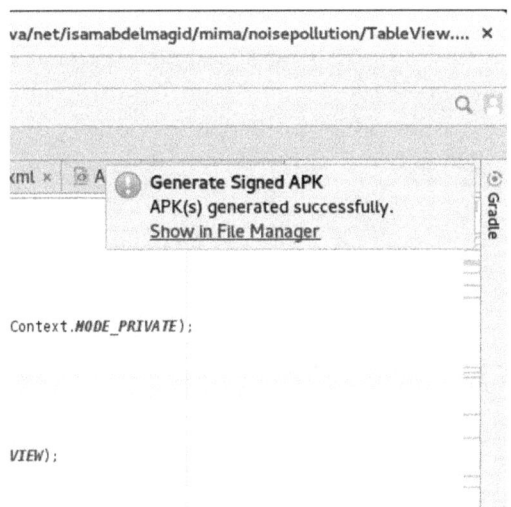

Figure 8.2: Generate Signed APK Message.

8.2 Creating a Google Play Developer Profile

You need to create a Google Play Developer profile in order to release your App on Google Play Store. To create this profile, you need a Google account. If you don't have a Google account, create one first at http://www.google.com/accounts.

Then do the following:

- Navigate to http://play.google.com/apps/publish in your web browser.
- Sign in to your Google account if not already signed in.
- The page on Figure 8.3 shows. Click on the bottom at **I agree and I am willing to associate my account registration with the Google Play Developer distribution agreement.** Scroll down and click on the **Continue to Payment** button.
- You will need to pay a one-time, nominal registration fee of 25$. Enter your credit card information and click **Purchase**.
- The page on Figure 8.4 shows. Enter the Developer Name which you want to be shown to users. Enter your email address, Website (optional) and Phone number. Click on **Complete Registration**.

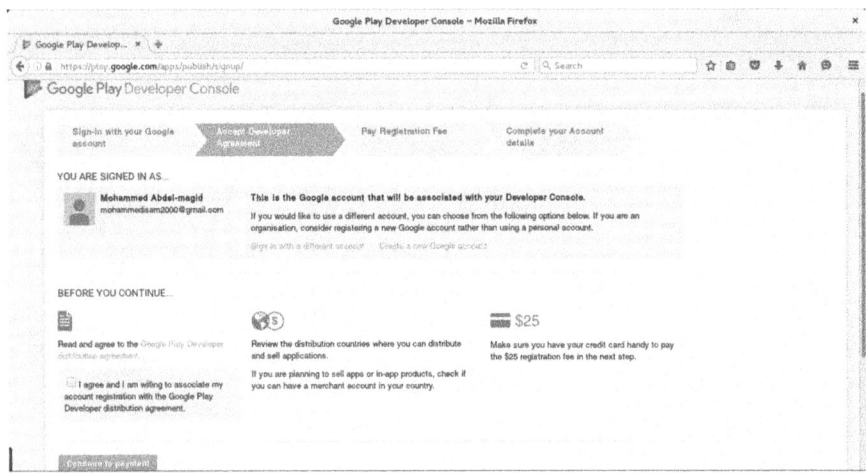

Figure 8.3: Google Play Developer Console Sign-up Page.

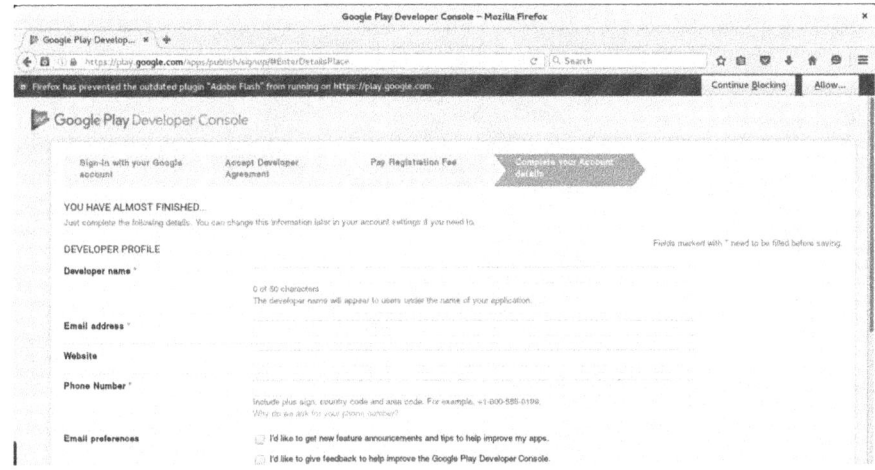

Figure 8.4: Complete Your Account Details Page.

Now your Google Play developed profile is created. While you payment is being processed (it may take up to 48 hours) you can start uploading your App.

In the Google Play Developer Console page (Figure 8.5), click on **Publish an Android App on Google Play**. The dialog on Figure 8.6 opens.

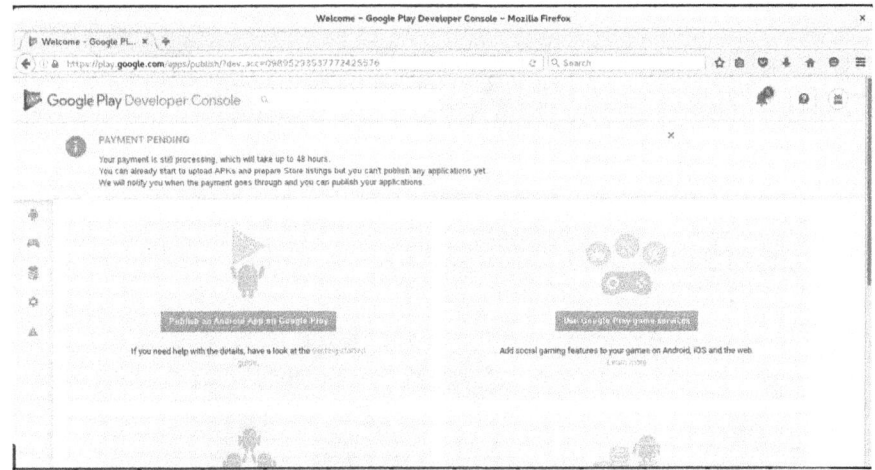

Figure 8.5: Google Play Developer Console Page.

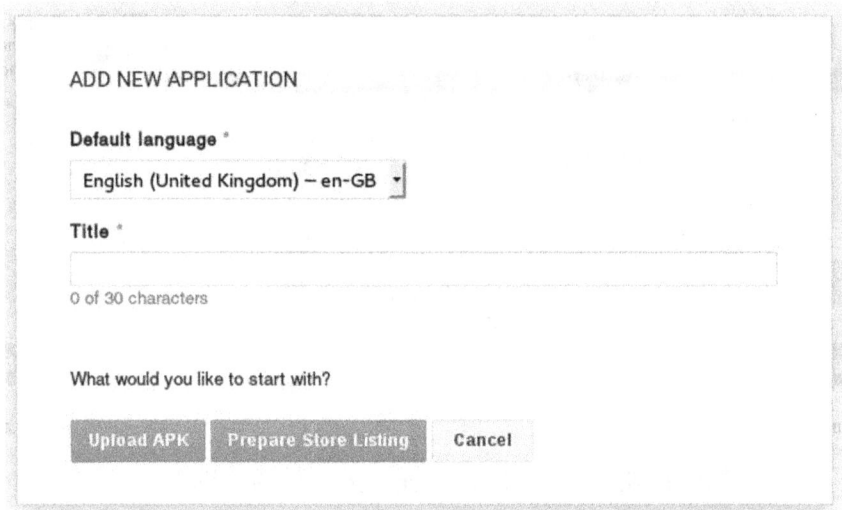

Figure 8.6: Add New Application on Google Play Developer Console.

Select the default language for your App and enter App's name. Click on **Upload APK**.

Scroll down, and click on **Upload Your First APK to Production** (Figure 8.7). Select the APK file you created through the Android Studio in section 8.1 and click **Save**.

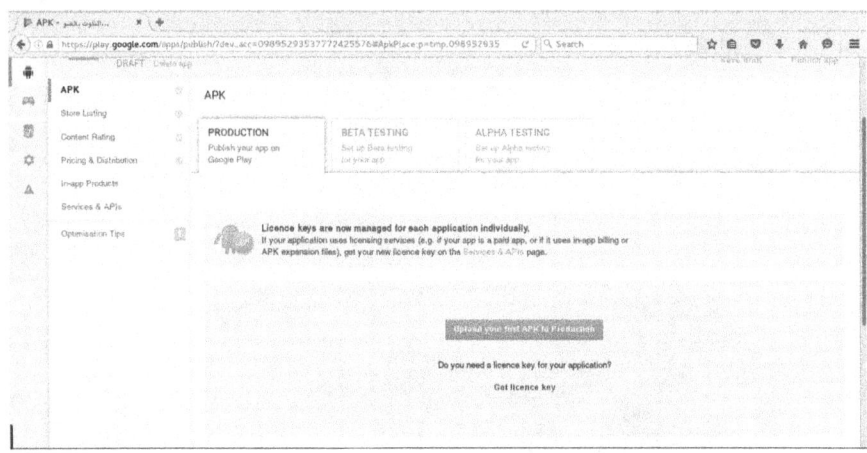

Figure 8.7: Click on Upload Your First APK to Production.

After the file is uploaded, you are taken back to the Google Play Developer Console page. From the list on the left, select **Store**

Listing. The title of your App is entered for you. Add a short and a long description for your App. This could be the book description you enlisted on your online publisher's site, for example.

You need to prepare screenshots so that users can have a look at your App before they download it. You can take screenshots from the AVD. On the menu on your right hand (Figure 8.8), click the camera icon, or press CTRL+S. The screenshot is automatically saved to your desktop. You can change this folder by clicking on the last button (the one with three dots) in the AVD menu. This open the **Extended Controls** window (Figure 8.9).

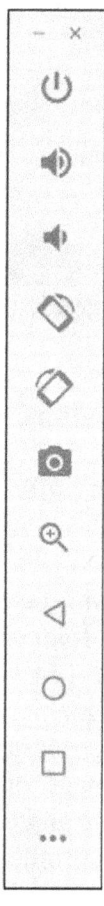

Figure 8.8: Taking a Screenshot from the AVD.

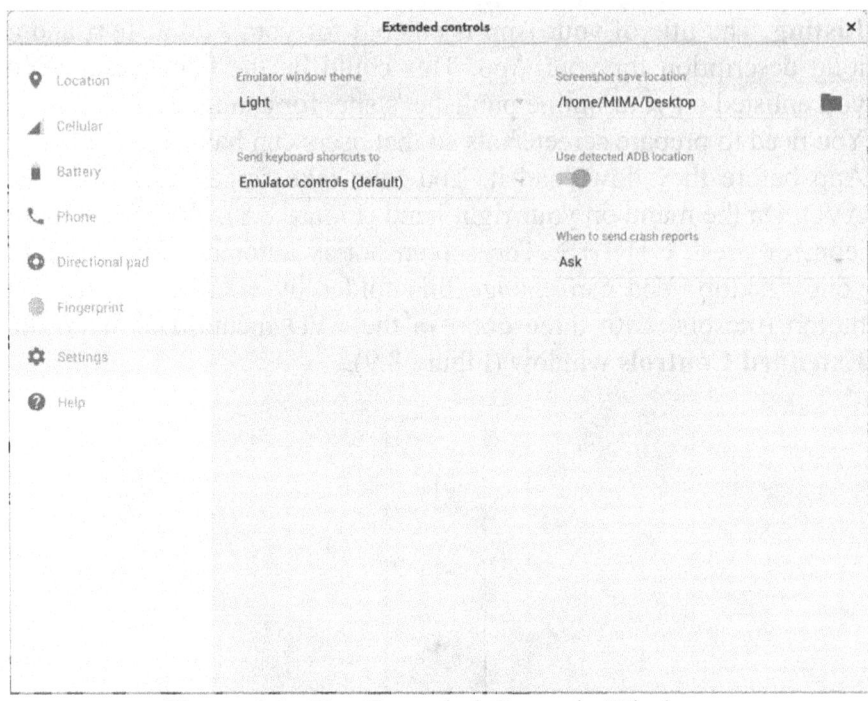

Figure 8.9: The Extended Controls Window.

Click on **Settings** on the left-hand list. You can change the Screenshot Save Location from the right.

Take a couple screenshots from different activities to show your App in action. You will upload these in the Google Play Developer Console page.

You need a high resolution icon. You can resize the **ic_launcher.png** icon from **mipmap-xxxhdpi** folder as I showed you in the last chapter. Make it the size of 512 x 512 pixels.

You will also need a feature graphic, the size of 1024 x 500 pixels. You can use your book's cover, or you can design a new image.

Finally, in the Store Listing page on the Developer Console, you need to fill in the Categorization and Contact Details sections.

Under Categorization, select the following:

- Application type: Applications
- Category: Books & Reference
- Content Rating: Everyone

If you don't have a Privacy Policy document, check the **Not Submitting a Privacy Policy URL at Current Time** checkbox.

After you finish, click on **Save Draft** button on the top-right corner of the page.

Click on **Content Rating** on the list on your left. Read the text and click **Continue**.

Enter your email address in the fields. From the **Select your app category,** select **Reference, News or Educational**.

Under the **Violence** section, select No (or as appropriate to your case).

Under the **Sexuality** section, select No (or as appropriate to your case).

Under the **Language** section, select No (or as appropriate to your case).

Under the **Controlled Substance** section, select No (or as appropriate to your case).

Under the **Miscellaneous** section, select options as appropriate to your case.

Click on **Save Questionnaire**, then click on **Calculate Rating**. Review the rating and click **Apply Rating**.

Click on **Pricing & Distribution** on the list on your left. Here you must decide if your App is going to be free or paid for.

If you choose to sell your App, you will need to set up an App merchant account. Click the link on the page to set this up.

If you choose to publish your App for free, click on **Free** button.

Select the countries where you want your App to be available to users. If you check **Select All Countries**, your App will be available to users worldwide. If you want to restrict your App to users from certain countries, select them from the list.

As our App doesn't contain Ads, select **No, it has no Ads**.

You can check the box next to **Google Play for Education** as you are presenting an educational material. If your book is not in the English language, you are not allowed to enlist it here, so remove the check. There are certain rules that Google Play Developed Console will show you once you checked the box. If your material doesn't fit the criteria, click Cancel.

Check the boxes next to **Content Guidelines** and **US Export Laws**.

You can review the documents by clicking on the appropriate links. Click on **Save Draft** in the top-right corner of the page.

Now you can sit back and relax. Once your payment has been approved, the **Publish App** button on the top-right corner of the page will be enabled. Once it is, you can click it to publish your App on the Google Play Store. Congratulations!.

8.3 Promoting Your App

There are many ways you can promote your App to recruit more users to use it:

- Encourage your family, friends and coworkers to install and use it. If they are happy with it, they can tell others about your App.
- Advertise in your Facebook page, twitter account, Google+, your blog and your website. Include a link to your App's page on Google Play Store to help users find your App.
- Create a book trailer. There are free and paid software that can help you create a trailer for your book. Search on Google for "promoting my book" to find some helpful hints.
- Send an email to your mail-list (if you have one), telling your subscribers about your new App and why they should try it out.

Those are only suggestions, use your imagination. The sky is the limit.

About the Author

Dr. Mohammed Isam Mohammed Abdel-Magid (MBBS, BLS, ALS, MRCP(UK), PgDip in Diabetes) is a graduate of the College of Medicine, University of Khartoum, Sudan, 2008. He completed basic training with the Ministry of Health, Sudan, then worked as a physician in the department of Internal Medicine, Ribat University hospital, Sudan, and the Ministry of Health, Sultanate of Oman.

He completed his higher training with the membership of the Royal Colleges of Physicians of the United Kingdom (MRCP-UK), and accomplished Post-Graduate Diploma in Diabetes from South Wales University, UK.

He tutored in problem-based learning teaching sessions in the department of Internal Medicine, Sudan International University, Sudan.

He is a registered practicing physician with the Sudan Medical Council, the Health Authority of Abu-Dhabi (HAAD), and the Ministry of Health, Sultanate of Oman. He is a full member of the Society of Acute Medicine of UK (SAM), the European Society for Emergency Medicine (EuSEM), and the European Respiratory Society (ERS).

He is a peer reviewer with the Science Journal of Medicine & Clinical Trial and the Pan-African Journal of Medical Sciences.

He is a qualified Linux system administrator, as he obtained the Linux Foundation Certified SysAdmin (LFCS) qualification in 2015. He is an experienced computer programmer with over 15 years of programming, with special focus on C/C++ and Visual Basic. He is the maintainer of several Fedora Linux Packages, and is an active contributor to the GNU Project (with his GnuDOS package). He is a member of the Free Software Foundation. He has designed and packaged several fonts, all of which can be accessed and downloaded from the Open Font Library (http://fontlibrary.org), or from the author's website (listed below).

E-mail: mohammed_isam1984@yahoo.com.

Website: http://sites.google.com/site/mohammedisam2000.

www.ingramcontent.com/pod-product-compliance
Lightning Source LLC
Chambersburg PA
CBHW071158050326
40689CB00011B/2168